Vet in the Country

RUSSELL LYON

Luath Press Limited

EDINBURGH

www.luath.co.uk

First Edition 2005

The paper used in this book is recyclable. It is made from low chlorine pulps produced in a low energy, low emission manner from renewable forests.

Printed and bound by
Scotprint, Haddington

Typeset in Sabon by
S Fairgrieve, Edinburgh 0131 658 1763

636.089

Contents

Introduction

KEEPING UP TO DATE with medical and surgical advances is a constant challenge to all veterinary surgeons – young and old. I'm sure it is the same in all the medical professions and in every walk of life. New thinking and new ideas have got to be evaluated, considered and if appropriate put to good use for the welfare of our patients. At the moment advances in gene therapy are exciting and no doubt will have a similar, long-term benefit for human and animal patients to that the discovery of antibiotics had fifty years ago.

Just as important from the animal's point of view are the improvements made in animal welfare. Many of the farming practices that I knew and accepted as a boy and young man growing up on the farm are now looked on in many instances as old fashioned and some now would invite the attentions of an RSPCA official. I have vivid memories of calves no more than a day or two old being taken to market without too much thought being given to whether they had been properly fed with their mother's colostrum. The common practice was to put the young animal in a hessian sack with only the head protruding. It was then taken by car (in the boot) or by van to the local market. The vocal protests of both calf and mother as they were separated were heart rending to say the least. The calf would be sold for a few pounds probably to a dealer who would then sell it on. The final destination of the calf could be many miles away from its birthplace. Many died after arrival due to infection brought on by the stress of travelling and lack of antibodies in their system. It wasn't that farmers were being deliberately cruel – far from it. But most young calves on a dairy farm were surplus to requirements and had to go. Farmers were unaware of the need to make sure that the young animal suckled properly in the first few hours of life to give it the antibodies it required to protect it from a hostile environment full of germs. Looking back I can still hear the bawling of the youngsters in the market and a shiver runs down the back of my neck like a cold drop of freezing rain. How grateful I am that such practices are now no longer allowed. Calves and most other animals can no longer be transported over long distances without regular stops for feeding and watering and are not allowed to be hawked from one market to another.

Other practices such as the docking of heavy horses just for the sake of fashion were banned when I was still at school. It was a heinous thing to do to magnificent animals. Quite apart from the pain and distress caused to the horse a tail is very necessary to keep flies at bay in the summer months. My partner Alec Noble described to me how it was done with a docking knife – a large guillotine-like instrument – and without the benefit of any anaesthetic. After the deed was done and the vet had survived the protestations of the patient, the remaining long hairs would be plaited over the wound to staunch the bleeding. I know Alec like most vets around the country was hugely relieved when the practice was outlawed.

It is such a pity that docking dogs was not banned at the same time. Up until a few years ago tail docking of young puppies by owners and breeders was common practice. It was made illegal but still the operation is carried out. Sometimes by vets who cannot see any harm in the practice but mostly by owners who exploit a loop-hole in the legislation. The Kennel Club could stop the horrible operation overnight if all dogs that were docked were prevented from entering the show ring. Dogs need their tails, and the public perception that spaniels, boxers or any other docked breed look better without tails has got to be changed.

One of the main driving forces for change in farming practice was the publication of the Codes of Welfare, which lay down minimum standards to encourage all stock-keepers to adopt the highest standards of husbandry. These codes, which have the approval of Parliament, lay down the five basic needs that all animals have a right to expect from their owners. These are 'freedom from thirst, hunger and malnutrition'; 'appropriate comfort and shelter'; 'the prevention or rapid diagnosis and treatment of injury, disease or infestation';

'freedom from fear' and 'freedom to display most normal patterns of behaviour.'

These animal rights are very basic and many ordinary people with no connection with the farming industry are now thinking and talking about these rights, which is no bad thing. Whether we believe in animal rights or not, most right thinking people will agree that all animal owners and keepers have a duty to care for their livestock in the best possible way. The Codes of Conduct lay down the minimum standards of care and ignorance can no longer be an excuse for mistreatment.

Having said that welfare standards and care are improving – they are – I would not like it to be thought that the way farm and domestic animals were looked after in the past was all bad. It was not. Many stables in the Victorian and Edwardian eras were much superior to those prefabricated loose boxes which are erected now. They were well built, well ventilated and well drained in stark contrast to many modern stables that tend to be flimsy constructions reliant on an open half-door for ventilation.

Because of the modern tendency for livestock units to become larger, employing fewer people, the tradition and knowledge of good husbandry is tending to die out in many parts of the country as fewer and fewer young people are becoming livestock farmers or earn livings as stockmen.

Farm animals are kept for food production. If they were not and everyone was vegetarian then the fields and hillsides would be bleak and barren places. Farmers cannot afford to keep animals for sentimental reasons. If they were not allowed to raise animals for food, there would be precious few cattle, sheep or pigs about and these would be only in zoos and 'model farms.'

Vets in this increasingly welfare minded age are often faced with moral dilemmas. When a vet qualifies, he or she takes an oath that states that in whatever dealings they have with their patients and clients they must put the animal's care and welfare first. But there are times when animals may be kept in conditions which are less than perfect but still quite legal. Sows in farrowing crates and chickens in battery cages are two such systems that spring to mind. A vet in private practice speaking out against a particular method of husbandry to an individual client will run the risk of losing the client and a valuable source of income. Most vets in this situation will go along with the method of production so long as it is legal but do their utmost to promote the care of animals wherever they find them, and try and change the system by other means.

I first thought of trying to become a veterinary surgeon when I was in my early teenage years, working at home on the farm. It was and still is a mixed livestock farm with a large herd of dairy cows. The cows had to be milked twice a day. It was a process that began early – just after five o'clock in the morning. It had to be this early as the milk had to be ready to go away when the lorry came, which was usually about seven thirty in the morning. It was not unpleasant to be up and about that early in the summer months even although this did not quite fit in with my predilection for reading half the night. Winter months were very different as they were invariably cold, dark and stark. The morning that crystallised my thoughts and seasoned my ambition was very cold. It was the middle of January. I was carrying a churn full of milk, about four gallons in all, from the warm byre (the milking shed) to the dairy where the milk was cooled and put into ten gallon cans. The route was along a concrete walkway, which that particular morning was covered in black ice. I made the journey many times as there was a lot of milk to carry and inevitably one of the times I slipped, fell over and the milk went everywhere including over me. As I pulled myself upright my hand stuck to a metal railing, it was so cold. I have never been renowned for my speed of thought even then, but in that moment my mind was made up. I could not and would not do that job for the rest of my life. I wanted out – away from the drudgery of the farm – and just as soon as possible.

I was fortunate to have a cousin who was a vet in a large practice in Kelso. As a youngster I spent many happy summer months with him while he was working. He was a quiet, patient man. He needed to be as he spent long hours and indeed much of his time visiting farms and stables over a huge area in the Scottish Borders. It was not unusual for his car to clock up seventy to eighty thousand miles a year. All his clients held him in great esteem and affection.

My main job when I was with him, apart from fetching and carrying and holding animals, was to open and close the many farm gates we encountered. In between calls we would listen to *The Archers* and the test matches and it is little wonder that I am still addicted to both these programmes. It was from being with him – Tom Rogerson – that I first got the idea I would like to be a vet. For a young lad in his very early teens it seemed a great job but a fairly unobtainable dream. Even then, forty years ago, the academic requirements to get into vet school seemed to be quite beyond me.

I was not thought to be very good with animals by my farming family. My elder brother John had a much better affinity with the beasts on the farm than I had although they knew to fear him if they stepped out of line. I can see him now talking to the bantams that roosted on the rafters in the small byre. They would talk back and then fly down and perch on his shoulders. I tried it and didn't have the touch at all, although looking back he may have been bribing them with feed as well.

I was given a young Border Collie to train to work the sheep. It was very keen to work and showed a lot of promise but in the end my father had to take it away from me before I ruined it completely. He reckoned I was too soft – 'kind hearted' were the words he used – to train an animal properly. My upbringing on the farm gave me a very matter of fact way of dealing with life or death but I could not bear to see any animal hurt or in pain and that has not altered as I've got older.

By great good fortune and a large slice of luck I managed to attain good enough grades in my last years at Biggar High School to get to University. I applied to the Royal Dick School of Veterinary Medicine at the University of Edinburgh and with the invaluable assistance of the head teacher Mr Shepherd, was allocated a place. My passage through the college was not easy. It was largely self-financed through summer jobs working as a crop inspector for the Scottish Department of Agriculture and by my father helping me to carry on farming in a limited way with some sheep and cattle of my own. I never had to pay for feed and very strangely none of my animals were ever ill or died. Or if they did, he never told me and just made up the numbers from his animals, which was much more likely.

After five years in Edinburgh I qualified – much to my amazement and relief. Despite being offered two jobs in Scotland I wanted to broaden my horizons a bit as I knew there were better-paid jobs and prospects in England. I had also the opportunity to go to Africa for a year to help research into tsetse flies and their role in transmitting Rinderpest in cattle but I turned that down as I desperately wanted to apply all the skills and knowledge that I had acquired – before I forgot them!

I joined a practice in Cambridgeshire. The senior partner was Scottish – Alec Noble. The other two partners were very equally amiable – Geoff Oakley and Peter Jackson – so I felt very much at home. Within a year I was married, a baby was on the way and I had been offered a partnership. It was a great start to a career in the Fens of Cambridgeshire and West Norfolk where people are as idiosyncratic as they were welcoming. It was a decision I have never regretted. I miss the hills and rivers of home to which I return very frequently but I always think the flatlands of the Fen have a grandeur all of their own. Even after more than thirty years they are still to me stark, gaunt and beautiful.

I am now a life member of what I regard as a dying breed of vets. When I graduated I wanted to be in a mixed practice treating all animals and that is what I have done throughout my professional life. I am a general practitioner who is prepared to treat any animal that comes my way or through my surgery door. If I don't know what I am dealing with, as does happen from time to time, I am more than happy to refer the case to an expert who in their field knows more than I do. But we are now in an age of specialisation. Young vets want to specialise very early in their careers and are often not prepared to compromise in any way. If a vet wants to go into equine practice, they will not want to treat any other species of animal. Likewise small animal practitioners would not dream of looking at a cow or a horse except in dire emergency. While it is in many ways entirely laudable to wish to become an expert in your field I believe in many ways young graduates are missing so much in specialising so early in their career. It is also making life very difficult for many country practices with diminishing numbers of large animals on their books. They are finding it very difficult to replace senior vets who are retiring. These are the people who did the bulk of the farm work and cannot be replaced. The result is many mixed practices are disappearing and are replaced by small animal practices. In some areas large animal vets are becoming very thin on the ground and those still willing to do farm work have to travel much larger distances to see clients. The situation will soon become intolerable. Large animal emergencies such as calvings or caesareans will not be able to be covered properly and animals will suffer.

It is a situation I could never have foreseen when I first started work as a vet and I am so very grateful that I went into the profession when I did. I love my job (well not all the time – it can have its down side). It has been hugely rewarding – not in monetary terms – and I would not wish to be known as anything other than a hard working and successful veterinary surgeon.

CHAPTER I

The First Patients

I EXPECT EVERYBODY remembers their first real day at work. I most certainly do. All those years of study were concentrated into the first sow I treated for farrowing fever and the first calf I examined with pneumonia. I was petrified I would do something wrong or miss a diagnosis of Foot and Mouth disease or Anthrax. And that was just the first morning! The afternoon was spent getting hopelessly lost as one bit of Fen at that time looked to me just like any other.

My first piece of in-house training was from my senior partner, Alec. It never occurred to me that the first thing I would have to learn when starting rural practice was that there would be times when I would have to catch my own patient. Alec took me out into the surgery car park and with the help of a ten-gallon drum as a target and a lasso, proceeded to show me how it was done. It was a peculiarity of the Fens, which can and does try a vet's patience to the utmost. It was a local custom which went back a long way. I came across the diary of a vet who had been practising in the area one hundred years before complaining of just the same thing.

It's not that the farmers were mean about buying expensive cattle crushes and other assorted pieces of equipment with which to restrain their beasts, but many just did not see the need for it when the vet could do it perfectly well for them. Indeed, in some farms one was judged on one's ability with the lasso. Extra points were 'awarded' for being able to whirl it overhead cowboy style and points deducted if you were actually unsporting enough to wait until the animal stood still. Now all of this can be quite entertaining if you ignore the patient's needs for the moment, and if it is confined in a closed yard and unable to get too far away from you. But it is quite a different matter when the animal is in the middle of a large field, which has no catching facilities.

The Fenland Washes is a huge area of land between the New and Old Bedford rivers, which run from Earith in Cambridgeshire all the way to the Wash, which is that vast 'U' shaped stretch of water separating Lincolnshire and Norfolk. The area is a wild-fowler's paradise; a bird watcher's heaven on earth and an angler's dream come true. It is also a place that veterinary surgeons dread. In the winter months that area is often covered in floodwater but in the summer time it is the temporary home for hundreds if not thousands of horses, cattle and sheep (plus miscellaneous birds – feathered variety) which are grazed on the rough pasture left behind when the winter floods recede.

An emergency call from one of the shepherds who patrol the grazing land, asking for veterinary assistance usually causes a distinct feeling of unease. Mostly when an animal is in trouble the shepherd will have it penned up ready for the vet's visit. But there are some occasions when for a variety of reasons this just doesn't happen.

My first visit to Welney Wash happened in my first summer at work. I met Josh Scott – the shepherd – at Welney, just outside the Lamb and Flag pub. He explained that a cow was having difficulty calving. She was located down in a field in a very remote part of the Wash and it wasn't going to be easy. Or as he said, 'thar's as wild as hawks master, I don't know how we are going to go on.'

This sort of statement I've found is never a promising start to any enterprise. I got into his ancient Land Rover and together we drove about three miles down the bank of the New Bedford or Hundred Foot River before he stopped and pointed to a field in the distance in which some cows were grazing. He handed me a pair of binoculars. I located the cow and assessed the problems ahead. The cow was a heifer – a young cow – and this was her first calf. She was lying in a corner of the field straining, and I could just see two little feet peeping out of her rear end. She had been like that all morning according to Josh and it was now mid-day. It was time for action or the calf might be lost!

We had two plans of action. One was to drive the whole herd

up the bank for the three miles we had just travelled by vehicle and pen them all in order to catch the one we wanted. This idea did not appeal to either of us as it might take all day and I for one had plenty of other urgent calls to attend. The alternative was to reconnoitre the scene by vehicle. The cows were used to the Land Rover moving about them – it was people they ran away from. We couldn't wait for extra help to arrive – this was in the days long before mobile phones. We had to resolve the situation quickly as the calf might be born dead if we did not.

Josh took the wheel again and I – like the fool I was – sat on the spare tyre, which was bolted to the bonnet of the vehicle, with my catching rope at the ready. It just seemed like a good idea at the time. But I was not confident of the outcome to say the least. We approached quietly with the breeze behind us. It is never easy to be accurate with a lasso if you are throwing into a wind. All went well at first. We passed through the herd without trouble and got very close to the intended patient as she lay on the ground. She was too intent on her own business to take any notice of what anyone else was doing. It was at this point that I made an elementary mistake. Just as I was about to throw the rope, she looked round, saw us and moved her head. Instead of waiting and hoping she would settle down again I threw my loop and missed her. She got up, the calf's toes disappeared inside her and she – suspicious – moved away. Josh started up the engine and we moved slowly after her and as she speeded up so did we. It soon got just a bit farcical. As we increased speed I was bouncing up and down on the spare tyre. I did manage to get the rope around a hind leg – don't ask me how – but I can report that the wing mirror of a Land Rover is no substitute for the pommel on a cowboy saddle. When I quickly wrapped the free end of the rope around it, hoping to slow the patient's progress away from us, it was quickly torn off and the heifer moved away at speed with a contemptuous toss of her head.

We stopped to reconsider our position. In the meantime the cow – I use the word advisedly – had taken herself off to the furthest corner of the field and resumed grazing as if giving birth was the very last thing on her mind. Despair and defeat stared us in the face but the heifer and her unborn calf still urgently needed assistance.

Despair I have found however, is often the mother of low animal cunning and another idea came to my fevered mind – and I was getting very hot!

Wash fields are surrounded on all sides by large drains filled with water and black peaty mud in almost equal proportion. We drove the heifer with much shouting and whistling and general uproar to the edge of the field. She could not escape us except by one way and she took it – as I hoped she would. She waded into the drain and got stuck fast up to her belly in very black mud. It was now easy. After all the lessons I had with the tin can I was pretty good with the lasso when the target couldn't move.

I got the rope on easily and we soon had her out on dry land with the help of the Land Rover to which this time she was firmly attached. It was fortunate for all concerned that I had along with all my calving kit brought a large container of clean water and anti-septic. Without wasting too much time I quickly got calving ropes on the two little feet that had reappeared. They belonged to quite a large sized calf. I made sure the calf's head was engaged in the pelvis and in the correct position for a safe delivery. I then connected the ropes to the calving machine. This is a T-shaped piece of apparatus with the horizontal part of the T placed against the animal's hind-quarters. The vertical part has a ratchet device to which the ropes are attached, and then with a lever tension is applied to the ropes to exert gentle traction on the calf. This has to be done carefully as it is possible that by using excessive force harm can be done to both mother and offspring. In this case even with the limited help available – none, as Josh was at the front end trying to control what had become a cow again – I managed to deliver the baby without too much difficulty. The calf was alive, soon shaking his head in disbelief at the cruel world into which he has just been propelled. Within a few minutes he was getting to his feet and taking his first few shaky steps. Before we left I gave the mother a prophylactic injection of antibiotic – goodness knows she needed it. We left mother and son getting to know each other and Josh reported later in the day that both were doing well.

Usually the animals that spend their summers grazing on the Wash have an idyllic, trouble-free time. But when a problem arises it can be very difficult and time consuming to deal with. I was just so grateful that this first time on the Wash, Mother Nature had come to my help enough to allow me to complete the job to everyone's satisfaction – including the patient, judging by the way she was enthusiastically licking her newborn calf as we left the scene.

You could be forgiven for assuming that it's only in farm animal practice that the vet is going to be faced with the prospect of having to catch the patient before it can be examined and treated. Definitely not so! Many times I have had to crawl under a bed to retrieve a cat, or catch a budgie on top of a curtain, and one of the strangest cases occurred with a dog.

The day I came across this animal, a shaggy reprobate of a Cocker Spaniel devoid of any brain material, it was near the end of my morning round. It had been a comparatively quiet morning, which had not been too physical or mind stretching, on a pleasant if dull day for mid-January. I had gone from call to call, accepting the odd cup of coffee here and there (with nothing stronger) and was contemplating what might be on the menu for lunch when my cosy complacency was rudely shattered by the crackling squelch of the radio-telephone.

'Vet Base to Vet Three, Vet Base to Vet Three.' Anne, our telephone receptionist action-desk girl, came over the airwaves with uncharacteristic urgency.

'Vet Three to Vet Base, yes Anne. What's the problem?' I asked. If I was honest I didn't really want to know.

'How soon can you get to Mr Flint's farm at Friday Bridge? One of the dogs is trapped in a shaft and they want you to get it out.'

'Which dog is it Anne?'

'Russell,' came the reply, as if it really mattered which one it was. Why they had to call a brainless Cocker Spaniel by that name (mine) I prefer not to go into at the moment. I decided it could be worse. Not one of my favourite dogs for obvious reasons but the Flints were one of my favourite clients.

'Okay Vet Base, tell them I should be there in about fifteen minutes; over and out.'

On arriving at the farm I was greeted by farmer Jim, wife Barbara and all the Flint family. This in itself showed how seriously they viewed the situation; normally it could take up to twenty minutes to find just one of them!

I was conducted round the yard by the distraught owners to the back of the end wall of the new potato store. A round hole was pointed out at the base of the wall, which was an opening into a ventilation shaft. The entrance was about two feet in diameter and was almost concealed by an elderberry bush, which had its roots in a muddy puddle. There was nothing else to be done but get down on all fours in the mud – thankfully I did have waterproof trousers in the boot of the car – and have a look for myself.

A requested torch helped me to see the idiot animal stuck about three yards along a wooden tunnel. How he came to be stuck facing the exit I couldn't begin to understand. If he had chased a cat or rat into the shaft he should be presenting his bottom towards me, as I didn't think even a dog called Russell would be daft enough to reverse into a hole like that. But well and truly stuck he was, wide-eyed with fear and whining in exasperation (or was that me?)

I sat on my haunches at the entrance and considered what to do. The shaft was too narrow and the dog too far in to be able to get anywhere near him with an arm or any other human appendage. There was no other way he could come out except the way he went in, unless we moved about five hundred tonnes of potatoes. The prospect of doing that did not exactly thrill me and I was glad Jim vetoed the idea as he said any movement of the potatoes might dislodge the tunnel and crush the dog.

'Mind you,' he said, 'how would it be if you injected him with a dart gun, and when he's unconscious I'll send in the terrier with a line attached. Perhaps the line would get tangled up with Russell and then we could pull him out.'

'Good thinking,' I replied, not wishing to be too censorious of a daft suggestion, 'but the only gun I have only fires rather lethal .38 lead projectiles.'

'Okay,' was the response, 'well what do you suggest?'

It was a reasonable question considering I had been rather quiet on the subject of alternative strategies. While I thought through the different options, Barbara took further silence from me for despair.

'Perhaps we should have sent for the Fire Brigade,' she said somewhat falteringly.

That did it. Spurred on by the thought of defeat and loss of face, the solution when it came to me was simplicity itself. I rushed back to the surgery for the dog-catcher. I'm talking not in this instance of one of my trio of nurses who normally fill this role for me but the more unattractive metal type, which consists of a long pole about five feet in length. It has a rope going down the centre of the pole and a loop at one end. It's a device we normally use for getting to grips with nasty biting dogs.

Thus equipped, I lay once more in the mud and with my arm and fingers fully outstretched I manoeuvred the pole near to the dog's body and then looped the noose over his bemused head. It took a few attempts but after much under the breath cursing I had him securely attached to the line. With Jim's assistance we gave an almighty pull and out the dog came like a cork out of the proverbial bottle – and without a potato being dislodged, which had been my biggest fear.

Now namesakes we were, that dog and I, but we had never been the best of friends. He had always kept a wary distance from me on any previous farm visits. But I do believe that on this occasion he was actually pleased and grateful that I had pulled him to safety. He came over to me and, totally unbidden, licked my hand. Even so, I did not trust him never to be so stupid again and personally supervised while some wire netting was fixed securely over the ventilation shaft exit. It was the first and last time I was going to lie face down in the mud for him.

As you will have gathered from what I have already said, the biggest problem that a new graduate faces is not the routine work for which one is relatively well prepared by one's education at Vet's School; it is the unexpected emergency which can test wit and wisdom to the extreme.

Fire is one of the extreme natural hazards that animals and men have to encounter. Wild animals, when a wood or heath land is on fire, can hope to escape by running in the opposite direction. It must be even more terrifying for domestic animals such as cattle, horses or pigs that are confined in buildings and often tethered. When a fire breaks out they are totally at the mercy of the elements unless help is at hand to release them. I have seen some awful sights over the years where, despite all the heroic efforts by farming staff and the Fire Brigade, many animals have died in appalling circumstances.

The first fire I was called out to as an emergency was at a piggery. I arrived when the worst of the blaze was over. Those pigs that had managed to escape were wandering around in a dazed state. All around was the stench of soot and burned flesh and the general debris of blackened timbers and burned walls. The area was covered with fire hoses and there was water everywhere.

My attention was however most drawn to a large drainage ditch to one side of the piggery. A group of firemen were gathered at the edge. The drain was steep sided and about six feet down before the water level, which I was told was also about the same again in depth. I peered over some shoulders to see a large sow swimming serenely up and down the twenty to thirty feet of the water-course. She was evading with ease all the firemen's attempts to snare her with their makeshift lariats made from fire hoses.

By now it was semi-dark and a search light from the fire-tender followed the animal's progress as she swam past. Far from being frightened she seemed to be totally unconcerned and was enjoying what for her was I'm sure her first ever swim. Apparently she had been one of the last out of the burning building, had dashed straight over to the water and without a moment's hesitation had jumped in. However, we could not leave her swimming there all night, as she could not get out even if she had wanted. We had to rescue her and a plan was hatched.

I was held by the belt on my trousers to stop me joining the pig by a team of men one behind the other, as I balanced precariously over the edge of the water. I had by now (what had become) my trusty lasso ready for her as she 'piggie paddled' past me. I missed twice but caught her on her third lap and passed the end of the rope back to the team. They very easily and willingly pulled her out despite her loud vocal protests. I gave her some pain relief for her burns and put her to bed in a well strawed hut that had escaped the fire.

It would be nice to report that when I revisited her in the morning her evening exertions had been proved worthwhile. Whether it had been planned or not her dash into water had been the very best thing she could have done to relieve the worst of her burns, but I found that her injuries were too extensive to treat properly and I had to put her down to stop her suffering any more pain.

Emergencies are always demanding, often frustrating, occasionally rewarding but often as with this case have a disappointing outcome. It was a hard lesson for a young graduate to learn. Despite everybody's best efforts and a successful rescue the patient still had to die.

CHAPTER 2

To Sleep – Perchance?

IT IS ONE OF the little ironies of life. I decided to get away from the family farm to avoid getting out of bed early and now here I was getting pulled out of bed at all hours to attend to other people's animals instead of my own. Somehow I had put the realities of late night and early morning calls to the back of my mind, although I knew a vet's job never finishes at six o'clock when the surgery door closes on the last patient. It is one of the hard things to which a new graduate going into a veterinary practice has to get used. It's either that or go and do something else – as many do. The reality of having a really busy day and sometimes hectic evening, followed by the requirement to get out of bed on a cold winter's night to attend a patient is just too much for many young vets. Everybody going into practice realises this but the reality when it occurs comes as a great shock to the system. There is little more likely to chill the soul than the telephone ringing in the early hours. It is comparatively easy to answer its summons through the day in a cheery, efficient and competent manner but it can be another matter completely when jerked out of a deep sleep or even a pleasant dream.

When I first entered general practice as a young and keen veterinary surgeon, I used to try and be as bright on the phone through the night as I was in the daytime. That wasn't all that difficult for me as I have always been a light sleeper and can almost sense when the phone is about to ring. It took some time for me to realise that answering the telephone like this during the night is not such a good idea as callers got the impression (no matter what the time was) that there was a vet in the surgery just waiting for their call.

Matters came to a head one night when a farmer phoned about

a farrowing sow. I answered with my usual bright manner even although I was asleep when the telephone rang.

'Veterinary surgery, can I help you?'

'Yes mate,' came the reply. 'It's Sonny Hill here. I've just had a look at my old Lucy. She's had fifteen lovely piglets but she doesn't seem quite right. Can you call and have a look at her in the morning.'

After making sure he didn't really want a visit until the morning, I gratefully and quickly for once went back to sleep. It wasn't until the next day that I fully realised he had wakened me at three thirty in the morning just to give me a routine message. He was genuinely surprised to be told (somewhat forcefully I have to admit) that I wasn't actually in the office all night just waiting for calls such as his. He thought we worked some sort of shift system. How all vets in practice wish that was possible!

From that moment, my telephone manner changed after bedtime and I now sound sleepier than I sometimes feel.

When I first joined the practice, a large percentage of the clinical work was with pigs. The most common cause of night calls was the result of farmers sitting up with their sows waiting for them to give birth. At the first hint of trouble they would be on the phone and, unlike Sonny Hill, they would want you there just as fast as possible. One such caller was Les from Welney, who died some years ago. He would never use the telephone through the day and would always get a neighbour or his mother to make the call if he had a sick pig. However, come late evening he somehow lost his fear of the instrument. This aspect of his behaviour may just have been influenced by the nightly visits he used to pay to his local pub. On more than one occasion he had confidently used the village telephone box and tried to reverse the charges.

I had been warned about Les's night-time habits but had never experienced them for myself. We had always been on good terms until one night about midnight Les phoned to request a visit for one of his sows.

His sows were renowned throughout the area for being the

biggest and fattest and most bad tempered. He kept them in converted railway carriages, which served their purpose reasonably well. These carriages were scattered at random about his muddy yard as if they had been dropped from heaven without any thought whatever given to their final ignominious resting place. After they had become too old and worn out, they were broken up and burned on site. On his return from the pub every evening, Les would check all his pigs in every carriage before he went to bed. This particular night he discovered one he thought was dying. The reason he came to his home-made diagnosis was the fact that normally when he looked at her she would unfailingly bark at him as only an angry sow can and chase him out of the shed. This time she lay in her bed and unlike me could not be roused! Very much against my better judgement, I got out of bed and travelled the twelve miles to his smallholding.

I found Les waiting anxiously in the yard and together we went to examine the dying pig. Sure enough there she was hardly breathing, oblivious to the world. I climbed in beside her and began my examination of her by taking her temperature; I inserted the thermometer into her rectum whereupon she woke up and ferociously chased us both for our lives. She had only been asleep all the time! I had always thought that Les fed his animals to the point of exhaustion and here at last was the proof. Fortunately she was also too fat to catch us, but it was a close call. After this episode, whenever Les called at night, my first thoughts tended to be how could I best help him without actually getting out of bed.

Over the years I have found I need to give myself little incentives to make me feel better about night time calls and get me out of bed when the phone rings. I have a secret craving for chocolate that I try to hide (successfully, most of the time). The only time I allow myself a treat is if I get called out of bed after midnight. The usual scenario is the phone rings, I wake up thinking vile thoughts – curses deleted or 'not again' if it has been a bad night – and then remember, looking at the clock, 'never mind I can have a bit of chocolate from my secret hoard.'

It was on a call to Welney that I first thought of my chocolate bar incentive. It was a quite stunningly beautiful moonlit night and I was puffing and panting my way up and down a five-acre field attempting to catch a cow. Peter, my client, had assured me as he always did when he phoned that I would have no trouble whatever in catching the cow. 'She won't move', he said, as she was much too busy trying to give birth.

He always tended to overrate my abilities with a lasso. I had been foolish enough once or twice to catch a cow with my first attempts and he thought I could do it every time!

Because of the full moon and clear sky it was almost as clear as day – almost. I could see the cow well enough as she wandered away from me – just out of reach. She gave me hope by never being too far away from me, but no success. I could see the cow but not the nettle and bramble patches as I staggered after her, rope in hand. My vision was becoming increasingly blurred by sweat coursing down my brow. I tried for up to forty minutes and for at least two of these Peter had been trying to help me. After this time I decided my chocolate tank was empty and the cow and Peter would have to wait until daybreak for my further assistance. I knew by then the calf would be dead and I inwardly cursed the client for relying too much on my unpredictable ability with a rope and for not having a decent catching pen in the first place.

Peter saw the situation was futile and said he would ring first thing in the morning after he had managed to trap the cow when she had her breakfast in yet another old railway carriage.

It was nine o'clock before he rang back next morning. 'Yes mate I got ur,' he said 'and she's tied up.' I ignored the implied criticism in his voice. Or was I, in my sleep-depleted state, being too sensitive?

Peter had got 'ur' well tied to a post by means of a sturdy rope halter.

'You know the calf's bound to be dead,' I reminded him, as he was starting to look far too cheerful. The little toes were peeping at me from the rear end of the cow as I put on my obstetrical gown and prepared the ropes and calving machine. It took only a few minutes to deliver it once I got started. The youngster was only just a little too big for the mother to deliver for herself and out it came with a rush after the application of a small amount of traction.

As it dropped at my feet, it gave a convulsive gasp. It was, against all the odds, still alive. My client was always known in the village to be a lucky beggar and his famed good fortune had come to his assistance again. It took only a few moments of vigorous massaging to bring the newborn back from the dead and very soon the mother was licking her new son; he was very responsive. Another ten minutes went past as I cleaned up, by which time the calf was on his feet determined to have his first suck at the milk bar – the cow's udder. All my Milk Bars were finished. Just as well as I was getting too fat. And the moon? Its malevolent presence had gone with the morning light and there was nothing else for it but to make a start on a normal morning's work.

After my night's experience in Welney I started to grade the awfulness or otherwise of a night call by my chocolate bar indicator. The litany of bad nights seared on my conscious mind and only mitigated by chocolate consumption now seems almost endless. But there were other times when I had only been out of bed a short time with a happy successful outcome, which made me feel guilty about eating any.

The worst type of call in the small hours comes when you are not on duty at all and should reasonably expect an undisturbed night. I consumed a whole bar not so long ago when I was not on duty and it was Fred on the line. Fred was one of my latest recruits to the veterinary team. He was a very experienced and hugely competent large animal vet and had been up all night with a mare with colic. Fred was convinced that the mare had a twisted gut, which meant we could do no more for her except put her down. The alternative was to send her to Newmarket where they had at one of the specialist practices – Rossdales – the skill, equipment and the large animal operating theatre to handle just such an emergency.

Unfortunately, in this case the owners of the mare had already decided to have her put down, as she was about fifteen years old. The prognosis for a successful outcome was very poor and the cost of operating whether the mare lived or died was a minimum of two to three thousand pounds and she was not insured. Fred asked me to come and give a second opinion on the case and bring the .38 revolver, which is owned by the practice for just these types of emergency.

As I drove the ten miles to the stables, still chewing on a Tunnock's Caramel Bar I remembered the last time I had visited these premises. The previous year the same mare had given birth to a stillborn foal. Everyone was upset for her at the time but we all considered – the owners and myself – that despite her age she was not too old to put her in foal again next year and hope for a happier outcome. Sure enough the mare had become pregnant again very easily and had foaled a good strong foal just a few days ago. I had had to remove a retained afterbirth from the mother but otherwise all was well. As I left the mare was looking happy and the foal was feeding well.

It was a very different scene this time as I arrived at the yard. There was much evidence of a long night's struggle. Fred's car boot lid was open, showing complete disarray with bottles and equipment strewn all around. Empty coffee mugs were abandoned in peculiar places and people were milling around with strained or empty expressions on their faces. I could hear the mare screaming for her foal from one stable and a little replying snicker from another. Fred had separated foal from mare as the youngster was in danger from the mare when she was in pain. She would suddenly collapse to the ground when the spasms from her gut got severe, attempt to roll, and lash out in her agony. She had been given large doses of the most powerful pain relieving drugs, which were keeping her relatively comfortable for shorter and shorter periods of time. Together Fred and I got the mare to her feet for the last time for a final confirmatory test of her condition. I inserted a long needle into her abdomen in a procedure known as paracentesis. This is to remove a sample of peritoneal fluid. The sample was bloodstained when we examined it and this was the last confirmation we needed that the bowel was indeed twisted. We checked again that the owners decision was final. It was – the mare had to die and as soon as possible to stop further inevitable suffering.

So Fred put her to sleep by injection as a last minute decision by the owner not to use the gun was made. It was not a problem to do it this way but it meant she would have to be buried in the very meadow where she had given birth just a few days before. Hunt kennels will not take a dead body full of barbiturate, as it poisons the dogs to which it is fed. When the mare was dead I took as much milk as possible from her lifeless udder. The foal was hungry and it would be some hours before we would be able to get a supply of replacement milk. I left Fred supervising the feeding of the youngster. The dawn was coming up – the sky was streaked with grey clouds flecked with pink by the warm glows of the rising sun. It was going to be a warm day but the sardonic cold light of the ebbing moon more accurately replicated my mood as I reflected on the harsh realities of keeping livestock. The chocolate this time had left an unusually bitter taste in my mouth.

The story, however, in the end had a happier outcome. After a few days Fred, who had been in the thick of things again, came across a little pony mare that had lost her foal. She was dripping with milk. The obvious question was put:

Would the owner consider allowing the pony to foster a thoroughbred foal? And if he did would the two accept each other? Within a couple of hours the answer was a resounding yes to both questions. There was approval on all sides, especially from the foal even if he did have to get down on his front knees in order to get low enough to suckle. He was a clever little chap – he had already learned to drink from a bucket – and the foster mum was a brave and kind little mare and it was wonderful to see the almost instant bond between them. Seeing nature in the raw now and then has its compensations.

Not all the calls during the night merit any more than two small pieces of chocolate. They may start out as emergencies. In many cases the owners are frantic with worry – hence the emergency call-out. The other night was no exception. The phone message said it all. 'You must come straight away. There's something awful hanging out of my horse's bum.'

I broke all the speed records to get there as soon as possible – well it was one thirty in the morning, a country road and there was no one about at all. I had been to the stables once already that previous evening to the same horse as she had a touch of colic. I thought then that it was due to slight constipation and I treated it accordingly. I must have been wrong, I thought, and inwardly groaned at the possibilities that might await me. Could it be a bowel prolapse? If so it would be impossible to replace and the mare was doomed.

The car and I stormed into the farm and braked to a halt with a flurry of gravel. I caught sight of the owners in the car headlights and they looked remarkably relaxed for a crisis. In fact they were laughing.

'It's all right. We know what it is and she's all right.'

Together we walked to the stable door and peered over and there was the mare calmly chewing from her hay net in the corner of the box. I turned her around taking care not to upset her foal, which was only four days old. There was something strange hanging from her rectum. It was placenta. I remembered now that we had been concerned about not being able to find afterbirth after the foaling. A colleague had checked her to make sure she had not retained any in her uterus, which could have had fatal consequences. It had been a mystery as to where it had gone but that was now solved. The mare had obviously eaten the placenta after foaling and it had taken four days to pass through her digestive system. Cows and bitches are well known for this practice – doing little harm – but I had never before encountered it in a horse. No wonder she had had a bit of stomach-ache that previous evening!

It was the work of only a few seconds to remove the offending piece of tissue and get back home. I even felt a bit guilty about consuming my two pieces of Cadbury's milk chocolate. A benign moon shining bright and clear over the sixteen-foot river should have been reward enough!

You could be forgiven for thinking, having read the last few pages, that all calls through the night are from farmers or horse owners. This is not the case. In fact with the depletion of the livestock industry in the area the most likely source of a night call can be from the police to a road traffic accident involving a dog or very occasionally a horse.

A police summons is usually routine and matter of fact with the call for assistance coming through a central control system. This relays a message, gives directions and only requires an assurance that someone will attend, with an approximate time of arrival at the scene.

One night the vibes from the message were just a little different. A mildly amused controller asked me to attend an accident involving a small furry animal. I was intrigued even though it was one-thirty on a cold windy night. I was also sufficiently awake to take a fishing-net and a thick pair of gloves with me. I didn't have to travel far – only about five hundred yards from my front door – to find two policemen looking decidedly uncomfortable standing guard over a car that had run into a tree on a perfectly straight piece of road. The driver claimed he had not been drinking and had taken a breath-alyser test to prove it. He had swerved to avoid a large cream coloured creature, which had run across the road in front of him.

'We have to believe him, because we've found it – there – look under that bush,' said one of the policemen.

I peered into the roots of the privet hedge and with the help of a powerful torch could just make out a pair of small orange eyes gazing up at me. Investigating further, I discovered a fully-grown male Polecat ferret totally unconcerned about the havoc he had wreaked on the highway. He was, however, quite happy to be picked up and deposited in the cat basket that I had also had the good sense for once to be carrying in the car. He was totally unscathed and friendly although the attending constables were not convinced. They were all for tying string around the bottoms of their trouser legs in case it ran amok!

I took Felix the Ferret, as I soon called him, back to the surgery where he lived happily for three days on cat food and love from the nurses until we worked out who the owner might be and he went back home to a more secure pen. I'm still not sure how the insurance claim for the car worked out.

One of the strangest night calls I ever had occurred quite recently at the height of the hot weather. A couple had, like most of us when it is very hot, been asleep with their bedroom window wide open. They had got used to their cat coming into the room as they slept but this night it was a bit different. Their cat arrived in the bedroom and jumped on the bed, as was his habit. But the husband woke up to hear an unexplained kerfuffle and scratching sounds. He put on the bedside light to check what was happening to discover their cat had brought another visitor in with it! It was a very large live rat. The cat, having brought the rodent into the bedroom, believed his night's work was at an end and had settled down to sleep. This left the rat bemusedly scrambling around on the wooden floor.

By this time the lady of the bedchamber was well and truly awake – unlike the cat. She sat up in bed and screamed very loudly. This probably woke most of the neighbourhood but not the cat, who merely stretched languidly and yawned. However, as luck would have it, the family dog was sleeping in the bedroom as well. He was awakened by the noise, saw the rat as the cause of the uproar, grabbed it and killed it.

'Wonderful,' said the husband, preparing to settle down to sleep again, 'what a good dog.' The lady would not – could not – go back to sleep with the body of the rat dead on the floor and demanded that it be got rid of – now!

The husband got out of bed and very gingerly picked up the dead rat by the tail and threw it out of the window, only for the body to be closely pursued by the dog. The lady of the house screamed very loudly again as the bedroom was on the second floor. Both husband and wife heard the loud thump as the dog landed on the hard gravel drive and then – silence.

The husband, aghast at his folly, very contritely rang me from his bed to request a visit for his dog. He could not bear to bring himself to go downstairs to look for him as he feared the worst and was very squeamish.

I said I would come as soon as possible but on the condition he went down immediately and looked for the dog. He carried the phone with him as he went for reassurance – still talking to me – and opened the front door. He was greeted by the dog, a large black Labrador, sitting on the doorstep, wagging his tail and pleased to be allowed back inside. I was party to a very joyful reunion. And the dog was none the worse for his flight, only sustaining a few abrasions and a bit of bruising.

Needless to say, the bedroom window was closed after this no matter how hot the night and it put an end to the cat's nocturnal activities. There were no more rats to disturb the tranquillity of the bedchamber.

I always dread the telephone ringing in the night when it is a colleague asking for help. We all need assistance now and again but when it is a fellow vet on the line it means trouble. It means a problem that has not been resolved or a decision that has to be shared. Either way my heart sinks when I recognise a fellow professional's voice.

Sometimes I can help without actually getting out of bed but all too often that is not possible and conscience gets me up to lend assistance.

I very nearly refused to go one night when Chris phoned. He asked me a daft question – I suppose he was a bit nervous about asking the boss for a favour.

'Are you doing anything at the moment?' he asked. I very nearly said I was but hastily reconsidered, because if I were I wouldn't be about to tell him anyway. After all it was one o'clock in the morning.

He was calling on the mobile phone from Welney Wash – yes that hauntingly beautiful, dreadful place again – and he had been there from nine thirty in the evening trying to calf a heifer cow. The calf was dead inside the cow and he, the vet, was totally exhausted from trying to get it out. I got directions from him, which as ever did not sound too promising. I had to drive off the main road down a cart track for about two miles and then walk a further three hundred yards to the field where they were. 'Oh and could you bring some fresh warm water with you when you come?' was the extra request. I was told I would see the farmer's truck and torches when I got close.

It was a dark cold wet and windy night and as I drove out of my yard I remember cursing the farmer for his stupidity of having a heifer which was due to give birth in such a difficult out of the way location. When I eventually arrived the poor animal looked as exhausted and wet and as miserable as everyone else. Not that it was easy to see anything much as the torches were beginning to fade. There was at least plenty of help – three others as well as the farmer and my colleague Chris. I more than reluctantly removed my warm waterproof jacket, donned my obstetrical gown and set to work. At least the water that I had lugged with me was still warm.

It was obvious from the instant I put my hands inside her I would have to attempt an embryotomy on the calf. This means, putting it simply, cutting up the dead calf while it was still inside the mother in order to remove it in bits. There was no way it was going to come out in one piece. The only other alternative was a caesarean but that was impossible where we were with virtually no light. An embryotomy is all done internally by touch and feel – no illumination required!

It is a long and difficult procedure at the best of times but the driving cold rain made this much worse that night. As I worked on with my hands and arms and instruments inside the unfortunate animal I remember thinking that the only warm part of me was my arms. They were that way as they spent most of the time inside the poor cow. And how the animal earned that unfortunate description.

With every groan she gave, and there were many, the farmer, who by this time was in great despair and distress for the state his animal was in, would disappear into the darkness. At one point someone actually suggested that he was thinking of throwing himself in the river, which was just over the bank from where we were working. I knew he was squeamish as he had – on another occasion – fainted while he was supposed to be holding the rope that was tethering a cow to a post. That time was in the cattle yard at his home. I had just delivered a healthy calf. I turned around to tell Jack it was alive and a bull calf only to find him flat out on the ground – unconscious. He was oblivious to everything but to give him his due he still held the end of the rope in his hands as he lay in a pile of straw on the ground.

The night seemed to be endless for everybody and it must have been an eternity to the animal. After I had finished all I could do was give her pain relieving injections and antibiotic and leave her where she was. There was no way she could be moved until daylight. I thought as well that there was a strong possibility she might have to be put down in the morning, as I was concerned that she had suffered too much internal damage to make it economic to keep her in the herd. Such are the hard, unsentimental decisions that large animal vets and farmers have to take from time to time about the animals in their care. When I rechecked her next day in the yard she looked better than the farmer and was eating some hay. He looked dreadful – as if he had a massive hangover. He told me that he was bringing all the cows that were due to calf back to the yard, as he could not take any more chances that this might happen again to one of the others. That at least was one good outcome I thought! The cow after two weeks to recuperate did have to go for slaughter. There was no other sensible economic decision I could make. My

veterinary colleague handed in his resignation. He had been unde-
cided before whether he really wanted to be a large animal vet and
that night finished him. He left the practice not long afterwards for
the comfort and comparative quietness of a small animal practice.

CHAPTER 3

'Pain or Champagne?'

AS A YOUNG AND aspiring vet I had, in common with all veterinary undergraduates, to spend at least six months, all out of term time, working alongside vets in practice. I knew one already – my cousin Tom, from whom I had already learned a good deal, but I had to broaden my horizons a bit and started working with the local practice who looked after all the farms in the area, including our own. The two partners in that practice were Duncan Robertson and Robin McCrone. They were chalk and cheese as people but got on very well and ran a very good country practice. Mr Robertson was tall and distinguished looking, and I learned from him more than from any other the art of veterinary practice. He was very skilled in looking after clients. Many could be difficult and awkward especially when it came to parting with money, which Scottish farmers always found to be in short supply when the vet's bill arrived. He was on good terms with everyone and behaved with a mixture of charm and good humour to which everyone, even the worst old curmudgeon, would respond. Going on calls with Mr Robertson (never Duncan) would tend to be one long round of drinking tea or coffee as we would be offered refreshments after every job. His first rule was never refuse a drink even if it was only ten minutes until lunchtime. He always said if you refuse once then it might not be offered the next time you visit – when you really needed one. There was only one exception to his own rule. We were en route to a farm to carry out some calf disbudding and castration. I had by this stage of my education become experienced enough for him to stand back and issue the occasional instruction while I did the work. 'Now' he said in his most urbane manner, 'we will no doubt be offered when we are finished a cup of tea and some delicious looking scones and cakes. Do not be tempted. Drink the tea without milk, compliment the lady of the house on her delicious looking baking but don't eat a thing and we might get away unscathed.'

It all happened as predicted. We did the work according to plan then sat in the kitchen; cakes and scones were proffered but declined graciously and we made our escape as soon as decency allowed. The explanation for Mr Robertson's unusual behaviour was that he was quite convinced he had twice had food poisoning after visiting this farm and he was not about to risk it again.

I also, as well as many other things, learned never to make a job look too easy. The first time I went to help him to calf a cow; he put his obstetrical gown on and examined the animal internally. He then asked me to do the same. I did so and he asked me quietly so the farmer would not hear if I thought there were any problems.

I was a novice but even then I knew if the calf was coming normally or not.

I replied equally quietly that I thought everything was normal.

'Good', he said 'you're right, just hold it in for a couple of minutes. Don't make it look too easy.'

I dutifully complied and a healthy calf was born a few minutes later. The farmer was pleased and so was Mr Robertson, as the vets had justified their fee.

He also taught me when carrying out any obstetrical procedure to always start with my left hand and arm first. As a naturally right-handed person this was not easy to begin with but soon with practice I became ambidextrous, which has been a great help to me over many years. And every time I begin with my left hand I think of Duncan Robertson.

Robin McCrone, his partner, was younger but just as tall and as lean as whippet. He worked very hard and long hours and I learned more from him on the science of being a vet, which included the art of observation. He always maintained that time spent by a farmer or an aspiring vet looking over a fence or a gate watching livestock was never misspent. It was important to recognise and be aware of normal patterns of behaviour. You would then be far more likely to see an illness or lameness in the very early stages and be able to do something about it quickly. This little homily struck a cord with me, as I was able to spot a few weeks later what nobody else noticed – a cow with a paralysed tail. I couldn't do a thing to put it right but I at least I knew what the problem was.

Robin also taught me what became to me my mantra – 'never show pain.' We had been called to a farm with a sick bullock. It was not that ill! It was in a pen and we had attached a rope and halter to the beast when it reared up and went backwards at an incredible speed. Robin had been holding onto the free end of the rope and got pulled chest first through the wooden paling of the enclosure. He grunted, went a bit white and then carried on with the job, first securing the animal more firmly again, then examining it and treating it appropriately. He was rather quiet for a few days after that but carried on as normal and it wasn't until two weeks later that I learned he had actually cracked two ribs against the pen wall. I asked him why he did not say anything at the time and his reply has stayed with me as my motto.

'Never show pain,' he said, 'it only makes you look twice the fool you were in the first place.'

It was my cousin who taught me to be resourceful under pressure. We had been looking after a mare with a suspected urinary condition and were very keen to obtain a urine sample. The mare would not oblige and we left instructions with the stable girls to have a container handy and collect some urine the next time she spent a penny. We returned two days later to find the mare no better and to make matters worse no sample either. Despite all the usual tricks to make her pass urine none had worked and no amount of standing behind her whistling and giving her a bed of clean straw seemed to help. She was urinating all right but not when anyone was around to observe her. We regrouped just outside the stable and considered what to do next when suddenly we could hear the sound of water splashing onto the concrete floor.

Tom dashed inside, whipped his cap off his head and caught the required sample. Then without pausing as the precious liquid escaped through the porous material he rushed to the car and poured enough into a sample bottle. 'Wonderful,' I thought, 'that was really quick thinking.'

He then, after the bottle was filled, threw the rest of the urine away, gave the cloth cap a few hearty shakes and put it back on his head. I realised then he may have done this before as Tom was as bald as a cricket ball and this just might have been a contributing factor.

According to statistics the veterinary profession is top of the list when it comes to professional people committing suicide and getting divorced and our consumption of alcohol and other drugs only takes second place to that of doctors and other health professionals. This will come as a surprise to most members of the general public, who have a view of vets formed initially through the James Herriot books and television series and the other TV programmes featuring celebrity vets and Rolf Harris. It is not the real world!

Vets still work longer hours than any other professional group and that includes junior hospital doctors. It can go on for years and years and takes a toll on private and family life. I was lucky in that my first wife did not seem to mind my long hours away from home. In addition I had very early in my veterinary life been blessed with two young daughters who loved to come with me on my farm visits even before they were able to walk. Carol, my eldest daughter, actually spoke her first words in the car seat while I was seeing a pony. Both girls were used to being placed in feeding troughs and hayracks out of harm's way while I examined an animal. They were also accustomed to sitting on a stool in the operating theatre and would watch emergency operations without turning a hair. The only time I did worry was when on one occasion I carried out a post mortem on a fairly large pig with my youngest daughter Kate (she couldn't have been more than five or six years old at the time) in attendance. I did it without giving the matter any thought until after I had done the job, and then worried about it for days afterwards in case she suffered some psychological damage or trauma. She didn't seem at all bothered and when I asked her about it years later she had no memory of the incident – much to my relief.

Most of what young graduates find difficult to cope with is the stress involved with the unpredictability of the work and the fact that despite their best efforts there are some cases and animals who will not get better – and some owners who, despite your best efforts, will never be satisfied with what you do for them. It's a hard lesson to learn but you can never please everybody all of the time no matter how brilliant you are as a veterinary surgeon. This, as I know all too well, can lead to dark moments and emotional pain when you wonder whether all the years of hard work and struggle to be a vet are worthwhile – for you or your patients. In addition to this, new graduates are not spared complaints from clients about fees or charges for medicines (which are mostly hidden from doctors and dentists by the NHS), especially when a much-loved pet dies. These same clients often find it difficult to accept that although they themselves are getting old, their pets (who are in many instances child substitutes and loved as such) get older at a faster rate.

The average day or week for a vet in practice is usually filled with work which rapidly becomes routine and, if you allow it to happen, mundane. I am fortunate as I find no two operations are exactly the same and all patients coming through the door or seen on a visit offer different challenges. Depressing cases do occur – sometimes too frequently but now and again come what I call 'champagne moments', to borrow a phrase from *Test Match Special*, when an animal lives when the outlook is hopeless or an operation goes really well and you feel you haven't wasted all those years of training after all.

Some of the stress I encounter, I have to be honest, is self-inflicted. I have a congenital affliction. I find it almost impossible to say no.

Some years ago not long after I had my first book published I was asked to go onto a local radio programme to help promote sales. I arrived somewhat late and flustered at the Kings Lynn studio of Radio Norfolk. But I was primed and ready and I hoped to deal with anything, and even had a couple of anecdotes ready if required. I was a bit nervous as it was my first time on radio but the presenter, Carol Bundock, was excellent and put me at my ease very quickly. It was just as well that I was totally unprepared for what was to follow. We had a quick five-minute interview on the book when the telephone lines started to flash. Carol said, 'you don't mind answering a few questions from listeners do you?' I wanted to say no but as ever what came out of my mouth was a pathetic 'yes – OK,' I gulped, 'why not.'

What followed were about twenty questions, none too difficult, about listener's dogs, cats and budgies with various assorted problems. An hour flew past – it seemed like only a few minutes to me and when we were off air, Carol leant back, smiled sweetly at me and said, 'that was good, can you come back and do it again in four weeks?'

How could I refuse? I did the programme for about ten years with another vet, Alan Slater, who talked about homeopathy for pets and I explained the conventional approach. Between us we usually managed to come up with an answer to most of the questions but we both dreaded getting a query on an exotic animal. Like most vets in practice I see my fair share of unusual pets, but I always worried about being stumped on something that made me look an absolute idiot. It happened one day just as we were about to go off air. The very last question was about iguanas and skin mites. 'Could I recommend a good way to get rid of them?'

For a moment I wasn't sure whether the caller meant the pests or the reptiles. I knew about skin mites but not the combination of reptile and mites. I only knew that iguanas could not always be treated with conventional medicines. I didn't dare confess on air that at that time I had only ever treated two iguanas before and that both had died. I managed to ease my way around the question and realised off air it would have been better to confess my ignorance but offer to find out for the listener and to call back later. After finishing a programme, it is a bit like just having made a speech and finding it received well. You feel mildly euphoric. It's a champagne moment!

There are many moments in life which start out badly and end well. Very occasionally a case which at the beginning seems to be hopeless finally comes good – much to the client's relief and my grateful amazement.

I got called to a little Welsh foal, which had been kicked on the leg the very first day it was allowed outside in a field with its mother. When I arrived it was lying where the accident occurred and no one was sure who had kicked it as there was two other horses in the field as well as the mare and foal. The right front leg was broken. It was a compound fracture of the cannon bone. It was not a difficult diagnosis as part of the bone was protruding through an ugly cut in the skin. He was a game little chap, trying very hard to stand up and at the same time calling to his mother, who was hovering anxiously in the background. The owner had very sensibly decided to keep him lying on the ground to stop any further damage to the limb.

The outlook for the animal was very bad indeed. I felt sick just looking at the wound, as I had to tell the owner that the odds were stacked against the foal being ever able to walk and run again. I had to say that I thought euthanasia was probably all I could advise unless they wanted to take him to Newmarket for a specialist treatment at one of the equine hospitals. This would be a very expensive option, much more than the foal was worth, as it would involve operations and inserting metal plates to stabilise the broken limb. I knew this choice would be very difficult for the owners. They did not have a lot of money and the chances of a successful outcome for the operation even if it went ahead was still very poor.

I applied a temporary splint to the leg and a Robert Jones bandage (a thick bandage with lots of cotton wool padding) and allowed him to stand up. He hobbled over to his mum and had a drink while she made little comforting noises to him. As it was now well advanced into a lovely summer's evening I promised I would obtain specialist advice from the veterinary orthopaedic experts first thing in the morning and then revisit.

The advice from Newmarket was, as I expected, not good. Plating the leg with steel plates was the only option in their opinion and euthanasia was advised. I conveyed this message next day to the owner and his family and my news was not welcome, to say the very least. Tears were shed.

'Can't you just try something – anything?' was the tearful request from the youngest daughter. I had anticipated this reaction and had given the subject a lot of thought overnight. I tend to collect old veterinary textbooks and rarely read them but I vaguely remembered reading about a similar case in a very dirty old book.

I suggested a way of treating the foal but I had to make it very clear that it only offered a slim hope of success, the odds were very long and it still might all end in tears with the foal having to be put down.

'Anything,' I was told, 'anything is better than killing him without trying.'

What I proposed to do was simple enough. The foal was going to be anaesthetised to enable me to reduce the fracture, which meant putting the broken ends together and straightening the leg. With that done I would suture the wound and pack the area with old fashioned sulphonamide powder and then apply a plaster cast to the leg. The job itself was almost as easy to do as it was to relate. The bone was set into a straight line without a problem and within thirty minutes the plaster cast on the leg was hard enough to allow the patient, who had by now wakened from the anaesthetic, to get to his feet. All that was left to do was to administer the first of daily antibiotic injections, which had to be done for the next ten days.

We all watched over the foal anxiously for the next few weeks. He was confined with his mother in a small stable, which stopped him rushing around too much, as he was in all other respects a healthy foal. He suckled his milk and pinched his mum's food with great gusto. The plaster looked more and more disgusting as the weeks went past but it was strong and held both broken ends of the bone in position while it healed. The only cause for alarm I had was the apparent contraction of the leg tendons, which caused him to walk more and more on his toe.

I left the plaster on for eight weeks then I was forced to remove it as he was growing very rapidly and it was getting too tight around his leg. It was plenty of time for the bones to knit together but I was more than a little apprehensive of what I might find under the dressing. At worst the leg might be gangrenous and all our efforts would have been in vain, or the bones would not have healed due to excessive movement at the fracture site and the leg would have to be reset.

I was right to worry but I needn't have. The skin had healed well and under it around the fracture site was a very healthy callus. I kept him in for another two weeks to make sure he didn't do anything too silly then he was turned out with his mum into a small paddock. I saw him three months later and apart from a slightly thicker bone compared to the other leg there was nothing to show the trauma he had endured. It was a champagne moment all right to see him cavorting around the field. However, the real thrill came nine months later when the owners actually paid my bill! According to friends and neighbours I was very honoured to get the money, as they were well known for never paying anybody. I must have made a big impression!

Most of the time you don't have to wait nine months for a glass of metaphorical bubbly. One of the last I had happened quite recently. It was six thirty on a Friday evening, the sun was shining and I was all ready to go out for the evening. Then the telephone rang. I was not on call but the duty vet was out and I had to pick up the phone. The voice on the line asked me if I would like to meet him down Whittlesey Wash (made a change from Welney Wash I supposed) and perform a caesarean operation. The invitation was cordially expressed and heavily laced with irony. He had no more wish to spend an evening in the middle of a field than I had.

A further explanation followed. My client had been watching a cow trying to give birth for over two hours. He had now decided, rightly as it turned out, that he had given nature long enough to work its miracle. Now was the time to get some help! The farmer was going to get his tractor and catch the mother-to-be, which he thought might take about an hour, as she was pretty wild.

At least that would be one difficulty solved. He didn't expect me to catch the patient, as is so often the case. Next job was to explain to my wife just why I couldn't take her out after all. It goes with the job but it is still a stressful moment.

The last job before setting out was to load the car with all the necessary equipment. Nothing must be forgotten for when you are miles from base a missing bit of equipment could mean the difference between life and death for the mother or the calf.

It was a beautiful evening as the duty nurse, Gay, and I finally set off in search of the action. The directions were all a bit vague. Come to the end of Eldernell Lane, over the bridge onto the Wash land and then turn right down the dirt track road.

I was then advised to follow the roadway as far as it would go and I would then be sure to see the farmer's bright red tractor at some point. Within a few minutes, there in the distance was the tractor with the patient securely tied to it by the horns. I had to make several detours to actually get to the place as the field was surrounded by a number of water-filled dykes. It was rather like a maze without the hedges as the goal could only be reached by crossing the right series of causeways.

Eventually after a lot of driving to and fro and much arm-waving by the client, we drew up alongside the tractor – on the other side to the patient. It was obvious from her wide-eyed demeanour that she was not best pleased about being tied up and could do some serious damage to my thin skinned car if only she could get at it!

She wouldn't have looked out of place in a Highland glen and had horns to match the hair; a real hillbilly! I managed with some difficulty to examine her *per vaginum* just to check that the farmer was correct and that she was in the final stages of labour.

Yes she was, the client was quite correct. The calf was coming in the correct manner, front feet and head coming first. But the calf was very big and the cow was so small in comparison. The calf moved its leg when I touched it and that decided me as to the only course of action. The farmer was right. It had to be a caesarean. It was the only way to get the calf out alive. With any luck the cow would be all right so long as I could get the operation done before the evening light faded too badly.

I started off the proceedings by giving her a pre-operative sedative. She did her bit by kicking me – with what seemed like considerable satisfaction on her part – on the knee as I put the needle into her. After that little episode I gave the injection at least twenty minutes to work before I went onto the next stage.

The operation site is on the lower left flank of the animal and has to be clipped and cleaned thoroughly before local anaesthetic is infiltrated around the site of the incision. It is easier to carry out the operation with the patient standing but in her case as she was so wild I wasn't taking any chances with her. I had given her enough sedative to ensure she was asleep and lying down on her side before I started.

With everything ready, both Gay and I scrubbed up with water and povidone iodine skin antiseptic and I made the first long sweeping incision. This has to be about a foot in length and goes through the skin, four layers of muscle and then the peritoneum. Only then can you gain access to the abdomen.

Once inside the beast, you have to take care to distinguish between what is the rumen, which is the cow's fourth stomach, and the uterus. It would be disastrous to open the rumen by mistake as stomach contents spilling into the abdomen would mean almost inevitably a slow death for the patient due to peritonitis.

In theory, having successfully located the correct organ, all the textbooks say that the surgeon has to bring at least part of the uterus out of the wound in order to safely cut into it. I have carried out a great many bovine caesareans in my time but only a very few times have I been able to do this. The alternative is to take a scalpel into the abdomen with one hand and make an incision into the womb, preferably over a foetal limb. This is done by feeling and holding the uterus with one hand while using the scalpel to cut with the other. This is exactly what I had to do this time as well and it is always a nerve-wracking procedure, as I'm never sure working blindly like this that I won't take a slice out of my finger at the same time.

Once accomplished – and for once not injuring myself – it was fairly straightforward to reach into the uterus, grab hold of the calf and pull it out through the abdominal opening. Only this time it wouldn't come. I didn't have the strength to pull it out backwards as the calf's head and front feet were jammed into the pelvis. I had to get the farmer to push the calf back into the uterus before I could grasp the front feet and then pull it out headfirst. It was alive!

The youngster was immediately seized by the farmer who proceeded to rub it down with a coarse piece of hessian sacking. He cleared its mouth and throat of mucus and made sure it was breathing before checking whether it was a bull or heifer calf. He knew the operation was going to cost quite a bit of money and was doing his damnedest to make sure he was going to get a live calf. Given the size of the newborn it was no surprise to find it was a bull calf.

It was natural break in the proceedings and I looked up from the operation site and took in my surroundings. The light was beginning to fade, which worried me as I still had a lot to do to finish the operation – but we had an audience! All the remaining members of the herd were gathered around us in a semi-circle and were taking a very active interest in what we were doing! Eighteen pairs of eyes were watching us intently. Thankfully there was no bull in their number although an oldish Hereford cow was doing her best to give the impression she was there as a locum. She was moving around in the background, pawing the ground and generally trying to stir up trouble. We had to move her a couple of times as she was threatening to wake our patient from her slumbers, which was the last thing we needed. The calf by now was on his feet and although very unsteady was obviously going to do well.

The second and last stage of the operation is much more arduous than the first especially for the nurse, and particularly as we were working against the clock.

Gay had to hold the uterus in the correct position to allow me to sew the severed edges together again. She had to lean over the cow and with both hands hold the uterus out of the abdominal skin wound while I got to work. It takes ages to do this correctly as you have to make very sure there are no holes left in the wall of the womb otherwise uterine contents will leak into the abdominal cavity and cause peritonitis and death. One layer of suture material is not enough and I usually put in three layers of stitches to make absolutely sure. By the time I had this complete, poor Gay was more than feeling the strain. Her back was aching and she had lost all feeling in her hands. But once it was done we could relax a bit as all that was left was to sew up the layers of abdominal muscles and then finally the skin. Just as we were getting near the end, the patient was beginning to waken up and the farmer had to hold her down by sitting on her head and neck to make sure she didn't get up and wander off before we were finished.

As I rethreaded the suture needle again for the umpteenth time, I glanced up to see the sun had set and a full moon could just be seen. It made my excuse of having difficulty in finding the eye of the needle for once quite excusable.

At last the final suture was in place but before we allowed the patient to get to her feet we milked a bottle of colostrum from her bulging udder to make sure the calf had a feed before we left them in peace for the rest of the night. We left mother and son to hopefully bond as a unit. He had at least got a full stomach of milk to see him through to the morning. If the relationship had not formed properly by then the farmer was going to take them both back to the yard where, if kept in close proximity they would both be fine.

I sometimes envy my human counterparts. Human surgeons have operating theatres equipped to the highest possible standard with plenty of staff to answer their every whim. They will have their favourite music played while they work and their brows mopped to order. But I doubt whether I would have changed places with anyone when I finished that evening. My operating theatre was an open field and I had music in plenty from the wild birds and the assembled audience of cows. Who need a glass of cold champagne when life is as good as this?

Whether I would have been quite as cheerful if it had been raining and the calf born dead I can leave to your own imagination!

CHAPTER 4

'A Cat Knows Which Lips She Licks'

CATS HAVE LIVED WITH and among people for many thousands of years and in that time they have changed very little, having until very recently escaped the worst excesses of human breeders' whims. They are remarkably self-possessed and mostly very independent minded. They come and go as they please in most households and if the family with whom they reside don't suit them for whatever reason they will in many cases move on and seek another situation that they find more amenable. This image of the domestic cat ties in nicely with the common belief that domestic cats are solitary and independent creatures and don't really need any social contact with people as long as they have a comfortable place to sleep and food to eat. However, this is not the complete picture, as many people will tell you that their cats are very attached to them and positively crave attention and affection.

To understand why cats seem to have this apparent disparity in their social behaviour you have to look back to the origins of the animal. The African Wild Cat is the main ancestor to the cat we all know. It is a solitary hunter and relies entirely on its own efforts to survive. It marks its territory as it goes along to keep it away from other cats, which keeps potential conflicts to a minimum. They started to become domesticated about four thousand years ago in Egypt where Egyptian society had a culture based on cattle breeding and rearing. Large grain stores were required to feed these cattle, which inevitably attracted rats and mice that in turn attracted wild cats who saw the vermin as an easy source of food. During some Egyptian dynasties cats were actually so essential for the economy of the country they were worshipped as gods. Over many years cats living close to people became more tolerant of their close proximity and became more and more tame. In addition the cat itself had to become more tolerant to other cats and learned to live in a group. The social bond that helps to keep individual groups of cats together seems to be related to the widespread rubbing which they do to each other and to us as well. They do this to exchange scent from a number of glands on their face and side and have a 'shared scent profile'. Any cats that do not have the same scent profile and are not related to the same social group will be chased off as any group of cats will only be large enough to share the amount of food that is available.

Feral cats living in clans are found in many different places: some very rural and others in feral colonies in cities and towns. They often exist quite happily in an environment that might be considered totally unsuitable by interfering humans. I quite often feel that many of these groups would be happier if they were left to their own devices instead of being 'rescued' and neutered. Unfortunately feral cats in healthy well-fed groups whether they are in urban or country environments will breed prodigiously until health problems arise. This I knew from personal experience as a youngster on the farm at home as there were cats all around the farm buildings. They were never fed except for some milk twice a day, which as vet I now know to be quite the wrong thing to give them. They survived by their wits and by eating rodents and rabbits and anything else that came their way. They were never touched by human hand or tame in any way although we came to know individuals such as the tortoiseshell matriarch we all called Granny. Numbers in the colony seemed to fluctuate, I presume depending on the amount of natural food available and on disease. No attempt was made to neuter the cats or treat them in any way but I do know my father would, if he found an individual cat in distress, put it humanely out of its misery.

In more modern enlightened times, many feral cat colonies can get badly out of control due to well intentioned people feeding the animals. This results in severe over breeding and a population explosion in a colony, to the detriment of all the cats in the group. When this happens local rescue societies such as the Cat's Protection

League or Cat Welfare, will step in to try and control the numbers by trapping and neutering the wild cats. Many of these cats when they have recovered from the sterilisation operation will be returned to the group. This can upset the whole hierarchical set-up in the family groups as castrated toms, for example, lose their status and position. Some, in fact too many, can't be returned and either have to be put down if unwell or if at all possible found homes on suitable farms where they can once again earn their keep by killing vermin.

It is women almost exclusively who run cat rescue societies and they are a dedicated band of people. While the majority of women who care and look after stray or feral cats keep everything within a reasonable perspective there are a few, and they are often unmarried ladies, for whom caring for cats becomes a life-consuming passion and an obsession. I have known quite a few over the years, dedicated people every one, but one in particular has stood out from all the others.

She was called Moira and she came into my part of West Norfolk about twenty-five years ago. She was a single lady, an only child whose parents had moved in the very best society circles in London. Indeed I was told by Moira herself that her father had been for a time a Lord Lieutenant in one of the Shire Counties and needless to say the family had been very well off.

She had been denied the opportunity to marry firstly by her parents who would not consider any suitor to be a good match. When she did find a man who met her parents' strict criteria he was killed in action during the Second World War. She nursed her parents through their declining years and after they had died she decided from that time on she would devote the rest of her life and money to rescuing and looking after cats. All her remaining frustrated love, energy and money was poured into caring for cats.

She moved up to Norfolk like many others before and since due to the attraction of cheaper housing to try and make her rapidly dwindling capital last just a bit longer. She brought with her from London, along with a few pieces of antique furniture and family silver, about eighty cats. I was never sure of the exact number and truth to tell I don't think Moira was either. They all moved into a charming period cottage that nestled into a high bank, which ran to one side of the property. This gave the house shelter from the north wind and also concealed a Roman road. It wasn't too remote a location as it was about a ten-minute walk to a nearby village and shop.

Moira was, by the time she came to Norfolk, a fairly elderly lady. Tall and slim, she had a personal charm that did not conceal an inner strength and a resolve to do her utmost for her cats, come what may. You could also tell that it was not without good reason that she was known as the Duchess in certain parts of London.

It was shortly after her arrival that I came to know her through a mutual friend who was also mad about cats. Moira phoned me and asked if I would be veterinary surgeon to her cats. Initially all was well. Together we worked out a programme for neutering and vaccinating all her waifs and strays, which were increasing in numbers almost daily. Her cats were obviously well looked after and well fed, which was more than perhaps could be said for Moira. All the cats were housed at least initially in a large barn next to the house.

After a few months it became obvious that Moira was losing control of the situation and her dependants. They were taking over. Her cottage became increasingly overrun with cats; wherever you turned there were cats. When you opened a kitchen cupboard two or three heads would pop out enquiringly. Turn round and pull open a drawer and the same would happen. There would even be cats in the cooker oven – just as well it was never used. Very soon the house began to look and smell awful. The carpets that had so recently been fitted as new throughout the house became sticky to walk on and you had to be very careful where you sat down. The initial programme of neutering and vaccination had to stop as Moira's by now meagre income was swamped by the demands of feeding her cats, who were increasing in numbers all the time as cats and kittens were dumped at her door. She never turned any away, which is why she was known locally as 'The Cat Lady.' Inevitably with so many cats living together many had health problems, which in some cases were caused by infectious diseases such as cat flu and enteritis. It was a vicious cycle. Moira could not afford to pay for vaccinations, which would have helped a great deal to counter the levels of infection and this in turn resulted in ever increasing levels of disease. Quite a few died or had to be put to sleep as they became terminally ill.

Moira would never allow any dead cats to be taken away for cremation and any dead animals would lie in state in her bedroom for up to a week before she would have them interred in her garden. She did this as she said she wanted to be absolutely sure they were dead before they were buried! As you can imagine, this practice enhanced the already pungent smell in the cottage, especially in the summer months.

After about eighteen months, in which time the cottage became more and more of a health hazard both to Moira and her animals, most of her money had disappeared due to the enormous cost of looking after all her dependants.

She was forced by her bank to sell the cottage, for a lot less than she had paid to buy it due to its now dilapidated state, and settled into two caravans at the bottom of the garden. One caravan was for Moira to live in and the other, with a large run attached, was for the cats.

All too soon the same scenario was re-enacted. Cats began to take over her living accommodation again and the conditions in which Moira had to live became increasingly squalid. To see such a fine old lady destroyed by her love of cats was very sad. She would pay no heed to pleas from friends, relatives or myself that she would have to change her ways and stop the cats overrunning her life. She would laugh a little but deny her cats nothing and not turn any away. She hardly ate at all while the cats that were healthy got fatter and more demanding.

Her caravan became the sort of place you put Wellington boots on before you went inside and just when I and everyone else was about to despair, a little miracle happened.

It was just before Christmas; a new caravan appeared on the scene, financed by some of her relatives. Its facilities were plumbed in and Moira promised all who loved her, especially the nephew who had arranged it all, that she would not allow any four legged furry friends within its walls.

That Christmas was for once clean, dry and warm. Unfortunately by the New Year her resolve had given way. To begin with it was only one or two that 'required special attention,' however the old familiar saga had begun again.

All her possessions were being sold in dribs and drabs to pay the costs of her animals' upkeep and she became so desperate for money she persuaded a local farmer to allow her to work in a gang cleaning and bagging carrots and parsnips. It was payment by results and inevitably, because her by now emaciated body tired very readily and her fingers were crippled with arthritis, very little money was earned.

Many people tried to help but any food that was given for her own consumption was eaten by the cats and I think she existed on very little at all. Efforts to persuade her that the cats would have to go or she would die looking after them were met with a fatalistic smile, which although it was never spoken, meant that she knew no finer way to end her days.

She nearly got her wish when she collapsed exhausted and was taken off to hospital. No one could look after the cats and it was decided, quite rightly by the local authority that the RSPCA would have to sort out the mess.

A very understanding inspector took charge and large numbers of semi-wild cats were trapped. Some were re-homed but the majority had to be put down.

When Moira came out of hospital, her caravan had been condemned and she was found a home in a local authority cottage in a small town about five miles away. She retired there with the three remaining cats she was allowed to keep. There with the help of friends she settled down well as the house was soon made cosy and comfortable and no more cats were allowed to be dumped on her doorstep.

Old habits died hard however and a stray collie dog she called Kim, who had lived rough on the estate, soon made his home with her. They became devoted to each other and the cats soon accepted him as part of the family.

She settled into a more comfortable old age but her concern for the welfare of animals in general continued. She would write and telephone politicians and church leaders on the subject of any current animal cruelty case. The Pope and the Archbishop of Canterbury were on her mailing list. She became very cross with one particular Bishop who not only would not listen to her but also actually put the phone down on her when she called once too often.

'Not very Christian,' she said.

As she now had only a few animals, I didn't see her so often but I continued to pop in if I was in her locality. One of her cats was called Susie, whom she always called a girl. He was one of the biggest, brawniest tomcats that ever 'walked the walk.' Moira could never somehow understand why Susie felt obliged to go out on a regular basis and patrol the neighbourhood. He/she would often come back with a bit of his fur missing and an abscess forming from yet another fight. Moira only got the message in the end after I told her that any self-respecting tomcat would have to fight if it was called Susie if only to live down the shame of his name!

On one occasion I called to see Susie just after he had yet another night out on the town. On my arrival he disappeared into the bedroom. It's not uncommon in my line of work to have to search a lady's bedroom for a patient and I was soon on my hands and knees beside the bed, peering under it. The room was a bit dark so without thinking too much I pulled a cord light-switch that was beside the bed. Nothing happened. But a few moments later a disembodied, even disapproving voice echoed throughout the small room.

'Are you all right Miss MacGowan?' It enquired.

I had pulled the panic alarm switch and it was the control centre in Kings Lynn enquiring if all was well.

Moira was completely relaxed. 'Yes,' she replied, 'I'm just under the bed with my vet.' I learned to be more careful with switches on cords after that episode.

Moira only had a few months in her new home before she had another fall and she became even more frail. Her lifestyle of cat caring and living in appalling conditions was bringing her to a premature grave. But she was very practical and clear minded. She made a friend of the local undertaker who called at her request to see her and made all the necessary arrangements for her funeral. She was positively gleeful when she told me what she had arranged. I for my part had to promise to put her three cats to sleep after her death as she rightly realised that to re-home her old friends would not only be almost impossible, it would also be unkind. I assured her that I would find the best home possible for Kim when the time came.

Not long after this, Moira died in hospital and after the funeral was over I went back to the cottage for the last time to carry out her final wishes.

Two of the cats were easily found and peacefully dealt with but I could not find Susie anywhere. My head nurse Janet and I searched all over the house without result until I remembered the old caravan and cottage days and pulled out a drawer in the bedside cabinet. Sure enough there he was in a very comfortable bolt hole. It was a very bleak moment, ending in that by now very cold little house, but I had carried out the dying wishes of an old friend. She had died as she had lived, putting the care and welfare of her animal friends first before any personal considerations.

From the very beginning when man first domesticated animals, there has always been the desire to change them. To breed bigger, faster, more aggressive, less aggressive – there has been no end to the variations human kind has tried to put into his pets, or horses or any other domesticated animals. Now with genetic engineering it is possible to make these changes so much more rapidly and not always to the benefit of the species.

Cats, unlike dogs, have until fairly recent times remained

comparatively unchanged. When the first cat show was held in 1871 there were only fourteen different breeds of cats on show. These included Siamese, Abyssinian, various long and short-coated breeds and the Manx. These days at any national cat show there will be up to thirty breeds and as many as four hundred and fifty possible variations. The search for novelty, which for so long was only to be found in the dog world, has really begun to take off with felines.

Some new breeds are the result of mating from genetic freaks, others are deliberately created and yet others discovered such as the Turkish Van cat or the Norwegian Forest cat. A good example of a manufactured breed that has worked well is the Bengal cat. Mating wild Asian Leopard cats with domestic cats produced this. This was first done in the United States for research purposes. The unwanted offspring were given away to a cat breeder who decided to start a new breed. The first cross animals do not make good pets, as they are still wild. It is not until they reach the fourth cross stage that the animal's temperament is suitable for domestic purposes. They are very good-natured and look magnificent – much bigger than a domestic cat – and are like miniature tigers.

Some new breeds are less welcome. For example cats have been bred without fur – the Sphinx Hairless. They were banned from being exhibited at cat shows, as has the Munchen, which is a cat with very short front legs. Most cat lovers would be very worried about the vulnerability of these and similar freaks but that doesn't stop some breeders from their search for something new.

If you are a cat owner, whether your moggy is pedigree, freak or a just good old-fashioned domestic cat, you will know that your cat is a wonderful companion. It doesn't need to be taken for a walk and you are unlikely to face prosecution for your pet making a mess on the pavement although your neighbour might have a few issues to discuss with you if your cat is using his garden as a loo. Cats fit much better into a small flat or house as well as a modern way of life. It is easier to go away for the weekend if your house comes equipped with a cat flap and you have a helpful neighbour who will feed it while you are away. It's not surprising there are now over seven million cats in the United Kingdom – as opposed to six million dogs – and the cat is taking over as 'man's best friend.'

They are wonderful company for older people for whom a dog would just be too much. Most of them will love to sit on a lap and be stroked and fussed over but of course only on their own terms. There will come a time when the cat will have had enough and will move away and do something else. There are also times when a cat will positively try to control a household in a very similar way to a dominant dog.

An old lady told me recently about a problem she was having with her cat. The cat was becoming positively antisocial – even a pest – and she rang me for advice. Every night when the lady went to bed the cat would wait until she had gone to sleep and would then jump on the bed and bite any part of the lady's anatomy that just happened to be outside the bedcovers. The answer seemed to be simple enough.

'Shut the bedroom door,' I said, 'and don't let it into the bedroom while you are sleeping.'

'I can't,' she replied. 'If I do that he sits at the door and scratches at it and mews until I am awake. I have to let him in or I don't get any peace. Then I fall asleep and he bites me again.'

I told her to try the water pistol trick. 'Pretend to be asleep and when the cat comes across the room, shoot it with a jet of water.'

You can tell why I am a vet and not an animal behavioural expert and she saw the flaw in this strategy straight away.

'He only does it when it's dark. How will I see him coming? Besides I'm going to get the bed all wet.'

I had found it very difficult during this conversation not to laugh. The image of the old lady whom I knew quite well sitting up in bed trying to shoot the cat with water was almost too much for me. Fortunately the caller, having talked about her problem also saw the funny side of things and we had a good laugh together. The simple solution was of course to put the cat in another room far enough away from the bedroom for my client not to hear it, and shut the door firmly. After a few nights the cat gave up and now both sleep peacefully in their own beds.

The practice of allowing a cat or a dog to sleep in your bed or bedroom I have little time for although I suppose it normally does little harm. I did however hear recently where there might have been a positive benefit to sharing a bed with a cat.

A lady was in hospital recovering from an operation. She was doing quite well until she started to have eruptions all over her body. These would clear up through the day but over night new lesions would appear. This went on for a few days until a doctor decided to do some detective work.

A friend visited the patient each night and morning. This friend brought in with her the patient's pet rat. The rodent slept with the woman each night and went home every morning – thus escaping detection. I was told the rat was used to giving the lady little 'love bites' while it slept with her and this was causing the patient's skin to break out in small purulent spots. I know that standards are supposed to be slipping in the NHS but this was ridiculous! I think she should have kept a cat in the bed as well just to control the rat.

Cats are amazingly tough and resilient creatures as I know all too well from treating them on a daily basis. Their hold on life on life is tenacious no matter what size or age they are.

A little kitten was brought into my Whittlesey surgery a few months ago. She was so small she fitted into the palm of my hand. She had been found on the riverbank, was soaking wet, covered in weed and deathly cold. I examined her and thought she was dead until I saw a flicker of the heart beating through the chest wall. The surgery was busy and I placed her on a heated pad and under a heat lamp. By the time I was finished consulting she was lifting her head and soon after taking her back to the main surgery she was beginning to move about. Gay, my senior nurse, took charge of her, called her Duckweed, and she flourished from that moment. She is now fully grown and bosses a household full of two adults, one child, two rumbustious dogs and three cats.

To me that is typical cat behaviour and why, as a species, they will probably survive a lot longer on the planet Earth than we will. We might need them but they don't need us – unless it suits them.

'If a dog jumps onto your lap it is because it is fond of you but if a cat does the same thing it is because your lap is warmer.'

CHAPTER 5

'Pigs are Equal'

AS A NEW GRADUATE and now fully-fledged young vet I was amazed when I started work just how many pigs were looked after by the practice. I had become a member of what was probably the largest pig practice in the country. This wasn't our estimate but was based on figures obtained from the Ministry of Agriculture, from whom we got crystal violet vaccine. This vaccine was used at the time to control Swine Fever and our practice vaccinated more pigs than any other veterinary practice in the country. It seemed like everybody kept pigs. Not only regular farmers with hundreds of acres of land and hundreds of sows but even people living in council houses would have a pig at the bottom of the garden. This was in stark contrast to the farms of home where pigs were a bit of a rarity and cattle and sheep were the predominant species. A consequence of this was that I had very little practical knowledge of pig keeping – indeed, I hardly knew one end of a pig from another. It meant I had a lot of catching up to do, but I was young and keen and eager to learn. I still am – well, not so young but still in the learning business.

Thinking back from a safe distance I can see now that even in the late sixties, people who had – in many cases – just a single pig in a hut (rarely grand enough to be called a sty) at the bottom of the garden were really relics like allotments left over from a war time economy. Things were very different to now, where some people have pet pigs such as Kunekune or Vietnamese Pot Bellied and keep them like dogs. These were proper pigs to be killed and eaten when the time came. This had many advantages to the owners, as they were a ready source of food when slaughter time came around as well as being useful repositories for the family scraps from the table. This latter habit is now illegal if the waste food contains any meat products. Very recently pigs in Northumbria that had been fed meat products in pig-swill that had not been properly treated contracted and then spread Foot and Mouth disease. The viruses that cause Foot and Mouth disease and Swine Fever often lie dormant in meat, especially if the meat originated from a foreign country. The consequences can be devastating for the livestock industry as was seen only recently where the infection started with pigs but became widespread in sheep before it was discovered.

It was not unusual however, having fed a pig at the bottom of the garden for some time, that when it came to slaughter time, the family couldn't bear to do it. It was easy to see why. Give an animal a name and look after it daily and it is very easy to get sentimentally attached to it. Pigs can be very endearing creatures. One such family lived in a council house in Whittlesey. They had a Large White sow, which lived on for years getting larger and fatter and she inevitably died as the result of heart failure. I had seen the animal the day before it died. It was terminally ill and I posed the question, 'what are you going to do with the body when she dies?' A blank stare followed by consternation was the only response.

On a proper farm the answer used to be simple. You called the knacker man and he would happily oblige and remove the carcass. In this case the only way in or out of the back garden where the pig was housed was through the front door into the hallway, through the sitting room and then the kitchen and out of the back door into the garden. To drag a huge dead pig (at least three hundred kg in weight) up the garden path through the house and out onto the street before somehow loading it onto a knacker man's lorry was clearly not a prospect that appealed to anyone. It was obvious that the pig would have to be buried in the garden and it took the man of the house and sundry (or was it surly) children two days to dig a hole big enough and deep enough to accommodate the animal. Needless to say they never felt the need to rear another pig and the sty reverted to being a potting shed. I bet the neighbours were pleased. Pigs, although clean creatures, do smell and they do attract flies!

During my early years in practice most people who owned a few pigs always felt the need to sit up with them when they were giving birth. It's a practice that has almost completely disappeared now as mostly there are only large pig farms left, and modern farmers who won't do it themselves can't afford to pay for a piglet babysitter at night. Modern drugs have also made it unnecessary, as it is now possible to inject a pregnant mother with hormones that will almost guarantee that she will give birth during the day. This is much safer for the animal, and of course more convenient for the farmer, but I sometimes wonder if eventually it will lead to a race of sows that cannot give birth without the help of an injection.

Being on call thirty years ago did mean that if the phone rang at night, the chances were it would be because a sow or gilt was having difficulty in farrowing. Occasionally, however, the problem was not producing the piglets it was the sow savaging and eating the piglets when they were being born. I am sure the deranged behaviour of many of the animals was due to being forced to give birth in a farrowing crate, which closely confined the sow, and being watched as well added to its stress levels.

The answer from the veterinary point of view to combat this enraged behaviour of the sow was to rush along and anaesthetise the mother until she had finished giving birth. Most of the time when she woke up she had forgotten what she was so angry about and got on with the job of feeding the surviving members of her family.

Not every farmer deemed it necessary to call in the vet to a nasty sow. Many used the well-tried and tested method of feeding it up to four pints of bitter or Guinness. Happy was the pig man who lived near a pub that would supply the slops from the beer taps for this purpose and not charge. If he had to have a couple of pints himself who could blame him? After all it could be a long night and a lonely vigil.

Another ingenious method of preventing piglets being eaten that I recall was invented by a Lithuanian pig farmer called Gustav. He looked after a pig farm quite close to the surgery, which was managed by a German. Both were wartime refugees and they did not get on at all. This may have been partly due to the German bullet Gustav carried in his hip as the result of being shot when he was in the army and fighting the Germans. It did not make for a very cordial atmosphere on the farm and many of Gustav's suggestions for the better care of the pigs fell on deaf ears. Gustav's patent method to stop sows biting and killing piglets was a halter-like system that fitted around the animal's head and incorporated in its structure a bolt-like piece of metal. When the sow opened her mouth to bite, the bolt would dig into her head just behind her ear. This in theory made the sow change her ways but I was never totally convinced by the efficacy of the system. Fortunately – or not, depending on how you looked at things, and these days it would be very much frowned on – the contraption never gained favour in the rest of the area despite Gustav's fervent advocacy. Gustav finally, disillusioned with pigs and fed up being managed by a German, went to Australia taking his patent device with him.

Domestic animals can be dangerous and pigs are no exception to this. When handling any animal it is as well to remember this as they all have their breaking points – don't we all! Push them beyond their limit and their veneer of domesticity will fall from them and they will become like their ancestors: raving dangerous beasts.

You are not too likely to do this anyway, but you should never go into an adult pig's pen housing a sow or a boar without having some means of defence or retreat. A boar in particular has teeth called tushes at the front of their mouths, which are like curved daggers. They are very sharp and set at the right angle to tear you apart with an upward toss of the animal's head. And I mean this quite literally. Many people have been cut very badly by boar's teeth and injuries have proved fatal in some cases.

This rule of self-protection is easy to say and just as easy to forget, as I know only too well. I had always been very wary about handling pigs – any pigs – but after a time familiarity deadens the sense of danger. The first time I broke the rule I nearly paid for it in a big way. I had been treating a sow with Erysipelas; this is a disease that causes the animal to have a very high temperature and generally feel very unwell. When I saw her on day one she was clearly out for the count. Her temperature was 106F and she had the typical diamond shaped raised skin lesions all over her body. I injected her with penicillin and she didn't even know I was there, let alone feel anything. I arranged to check her the next day. On my return visit I was unable to find the owner so I went to the pen and found her for myself. She was still sound asleep just as I had left her the day before. I got in beside her, looked at her properly, took her temperature again, which I noted with satisfaction had returned to normal, and still she slept on. I decided to give her another injection. I filled the syringe and jabbed it into her rear end. That was as far as I got. She leapt to her feet screaming with outrage and came for me with a wicked gleam in her eye and malicious intent. The pen door was locked, there was no one about and I had not taken the usual precaution of having a pig board with me, which serves as a protective barrier. All I had was my medicine bag full of drugs and medicines and as I leapt for safety over the wall of the pen I thrust it into her open mouth. It gave me just enough time to get out of her reach but didn't do a lot for the contents of the bag. They were strewn and broken all over her pen and it taught me an expensive lesson I have never forgotten.

Farrowing time is probably the most stressful time for the pig keeper and the animals he or she is looking after. But whether a pig farm becomes and remains viable depends on the other end of the natural cycle – procreation. It used to be sufficient to allow newly weaned sows to run with a boar and let nature take its natural course. On a modern pig farm this is never allowed to happen. Boars and sows are separate from each other except for the act of mating although they are allowed to get thoroughly frustrated first. They are kept within sight and smell of each other, which gets both parties ready for action when the time is right. The pig man first checks that the sow is fully in season and ready for the boar by pressing down on her back with both hands or sometimes actually sitting on her back. If she gives every indication of liking this activity by standing with all four feet firmly anchored to the ground, she is deemed to be ready. Boar and sow are then allowed to meet and a little foreplay is permitted, fully supervised of course. Normally the boar will make the entire running with teeth chomping and much salivating, interspersed with the occasional playful nudge into the sow's ribs. This last little habit can damage the sow quite badly if his tushes are long and sharp. A boar with this tendency has to have his teeth cut short, which is not the most pleasant procedure for either boar or vet.

When foreplay gives way to the full act, it is even more essential that the lovers are still watched very carefully. It is not uncommon for a boar to be mounted and giving every appearance of satisfaction, when his energies are being directed into quite the wrong orifice. This doesn't, as you will imagine, do a lot for conception rates. Normally what comes naturally comes problem free, but the pig keeper has to be careful about selecting the right mate for the sow. If a young inexperienced boar is put with an old sow and he shows his inexperience by being clumsy, she is quite likely to turn on him, give him a good beating and put him off sex for life. Equally, an old heavy boar can badly hurt a young, small gilt by overly robust behaviour.

It is very common now to avoid these difficulties and also the cost of keeping boars by using artificial insemination (AI) on the sows to get them pregnant. The same principles are used to check whether the sow is in season and this is often augmented with a burst of boar odour from an aerosol can. A rubber or plastic catheter is placed in the sow's vagina, which closely resembles a boar's penis. It is one of these objects in which reality is stranger than fiction, as a boar's penis at its furthest extremity resembles a corkscrew. When a sow is full in season and receptive this spiral shaped arrangement – if you will pardon the expression – screws into the sow's cervix and locks in position. When AI first began to be used commonly my colleagues and I would spend quite a lot of time demonstrating the technique to local farmers and small holders. One farmer in particular was very anxious to learn the method but was not very patient. When the catheter is in the correct position the bottle of the semen is attached and the liquid is then allowed to drain by gravity into the sow. This process can be time consuming and can take up to thirty minutes to accomplish. I demonstrated this with the first sow but when it came to be his turn with the next animal, he couldn't resist squeezing the plastic bottle to hurry the process along. By so doing half the quantity of semen was ejected from the sow. I of course put him right, told him the error of his ways and said he would be very lucky to get any piglets from this animal, or at best a much reduced litter number. I made the mistake of noting which was his sow and which was mine. In due time when the piglets arrived, my sow has six and his had fifteen. Thereafter he stuck to his own technique – so much for the expert!

I am often struck by the many things that pigs and Homo Sapiens have in common. The first similarity occurs with birth. We are, like them, born naked, without body hair and defenceless, and arrive into a world where we have to depend on others for warmth and food. Despite this handicap they are, like us, very successful as a species and there are about eight hundred million pigs in the world at any one time, nearly half of these in Asia. This is probably due to the fact that pigs are a major source of meat in most countries, with the notable exception of Muslim, Hindu and Jewish cultures.

While it is true that human mothers seldom have more than one or two children at the same time (unless the mothers are having fertility treatment) and sows usually have at least ten piglets each time they give birth, further parallels can be drawn. Sows under modern pig husbandry systems are confined in farrowing crates when they give birth. These are tubular metal structures, which allow the sow to stand and lie down comfortably enough but not to turn around.

They are used for two main reasons. In the first place they were developed for the convenience of the pig keeper. As I have already said any animal when stressed can be aggressive. This is especially the case when a sow is farrowing and the expectant mothers can become very irritable when they are giving birth, particularly if they are having difficulties passing their piglets. It is so much easier to attend to them while they are so confined, without the worry of possibly being attacked. It is also safer and much easier to handle any youngsters, which may require medical attention. Piglets do squeal when they are being handled and the sow, like any good mother, will leap to their defence if she thinks her offspring are in danger. Secondly – and most pig farmers would put this first in their reasons for confining sows – the use of farrowing pens will dramatically reduce the incidence of piglet deaths by crushing, due to being laid upon by clumsy mothers.

To confine an animal while she is trying to give birth makes the whole process much more difficult for the mother. This is not my field but having had two daughters I know that most women find that lying down and being confined, often with legs in harness, both delays and impedes the natural birth process. Not only that but labour wards, at least when my children were born, had very bright lighting and often a lack of privacy, which was not conducive to an easy labour. It now is realised that it is much more natural to be able to walk around, even use a birthing pool, until the birth is very imminent. And how much more natural it is to have the baby at home in familiar surroundings with subdued lighting and just a trusted midwife in attendance. So it is with sows. The incidence of dystocia (birthing problems) is vastly reduced under the new modern outdoor system of husbandry where each sow – instead of being confined in a farrowing crate in a large, brightly lit room, with many other sows in identical crates – has her own private ark or farrowing hut. They snuggle into their own quarters and make a bed with straw and very seldom have problems giving birth. These huts are well insulated – warm in winter and cool in summer. The only extra requirement in the winter months is a plastic curtain across the door to keep out draughts. Piglets born and reared indoors have to have artificial heating to keep them alive and healthy. Not so in the outdoor farrowing hut. The heat generated by the sow's body coupled with the insulation in the building keeps them, even when there is snow on the ground, as warm as toast. It is a very natural environment and closely mimics what the sow would arrange for herself given the chance.

Some situations and some climates make outdoor pig production impossible. If ground is badly drained and would turn into a quagmire around the arks then clearly the pigs would not be very comfortable. Similarly if the field were very exposed to the worst of weather, such as half way up a hillside in the north of Scotland then it clearly would not work. But it is entirely practical to mimic outdoor pig housing conditions inside so that the mothers have individual pens, which allow them to exercise at will. Some old fashioned units that I remember from thirty years ago managed to do this very successfully. Unfortunately most of these have gone as they proved to be very expensive to manage in time and labour and were replaced by large sheds filled with row upon row of farrowing crates. The problem is that to compete with pig farms on the continent, farmers must produce pigs as cheaply as possible and the mass housing of pigs indoors takes up too much space and is not cost effective.

Most people, even inveterate townies, are aware just how much fun young lambs have playing and frolicking and what a delight it is to watch them. Young pigs reared outdoors have just as much fun as lambs. They delight in chasing games and even when conditions are wet and cold (once they are old enough to be allowed out of the farrowing ark) they will go out to play like any human youngster. Young piglets are kept inside a hut by means of a fender at the door until the farmer is sure they are old enough to find their way back to the right house. When they are allowed out it is almost like young children needing to work off excess energy after being closely confined. They rush around like demented puppies, playing and exploring at the same time.

Pigs, like most people, love to sunbathe and it can be very common in the summer with outdoor pigs to have the whole herd badly sunburned. This can make the pigs very uncomfortable and their skin goes red and peels just as it does with us. Too much sun can also cause abortions and general infertility so the farmer must provide good shade for his pigs. That is not to say that all the pigs will be sensible enough to use the shade provided. Many will still lie out luxuriating in the warmth of the sun. To get around this the farmer has to provide natural suntan lotion – mud! Pigs living outdoors in the summer must have access to mud wallows. These are shallow holes in the ground scooped out by diggers and filled with water. Sows will happily lie side by side like hippopotami, in a wallow, all day – luxuriating in the warmth and sociability and pleasantness of life. They get covered in mud at the same time, which protects them from the sun. Farmers have to be careful not to allow heavily pregnant sows access to the wallows, as some would use it as a 'birthing pool' and give birth in the quagmire – in which case most of the piglets would drown. And I've seen that happen.

Wallows should be drained and the location changed regularly, and the same wallow should not be used as a pond year after year as they can be a source of infection and a means by which disease can be transmitted from one pig to another. Outbreaks of infertility can sometimes be traced to bacteria such as Leptospirosis (most commonly carried by rats), which will exist quite happily in the mud and water waiting for the next unsuspecting victim to come along and get infected.

Unfortunately, there has not yet been devised a system of management which will allow pigs to be fattened for market while still keeping them outdoors. After piglets are weaned they will, if they are lucky, be transferred to large straw-filled pens. There they will be fed a cereal-based meal, mixed with water to appear like porridge. Many, however, will be kept in fattening units, which have no straw and are fed on nuts or dry meal. If they are unfortunate enough to be overcrowded as well then many of the social vices will erupt. Bullying, tail biting, ear sucking and even cannibalism can happen if living conditions are poor. Most pig farmers are well aware of these problems and provide 'toys' such as footballs and other objects for the pigs to play with to try and prevent boredom. The similarities between crowded pigs behaving badly and football hooligans are rather obvious. The better you treat pigs and people, the better in turn they will behave – or in other words as the old adage says, 'look after your animals and they will look after you.'

Pig and human stomachs are very similar in size and are subject to the same disorders. Ulcers are just as common in pigs as they are in people and it is thought that stress induced by overcrowding, travel and mixing with strangers are all predisposing factors in pigs. The obvious parallel with people can again be drawn. Unlike people, pigs seldom receive treatment for gastric ulceration. Often the first the farmer will know is when a pig dies and a post mortem reveals a hole in the stomach wall and peritonitis as the result of stomach contents reaching the abdominal cavity. Prevention is much more important to the pig keeper than treatment and although the cases of gastric ulceration are now thought to be caused in many instances by specific bacterial infection, there is no doubt that the stress – however that is defined – that pigs and people meet in the modern world contributes in no small way to the onset of symptoms. Diet for the pig, like us, is very important and a ration that has a high fibre content is very useful in maintaining a healthy gut and may help prevent gastric ulcers.

Transplantation surgery for people has now become commonplace. The exchange of hearts, lungs, livers and kidneys between victims of sudden death and patients requiring a new organ are now such a part of life and death that they occur almost without comment. But there are never enough donated organs to supply an ever-increasing demand. Attempts are being made to get round this by using pig organs such as hearts and livers instead of human donor organs. I can see no ethical objections to this, as it seems no worse than rearing pigs to eat them. The mechanics of a heart transplant operation are relatively straightforward as human and pig hearts are very similar in shape and size. The main problem occurs with rejection of the alien heart as foreign material. Anti-rejection drugs are not yet good enough to stop this from happening. However, pigs are now being bred with some human genes, which will ensure that sometime in the near future, rejection will cease to be such a problem and people will live when they might otherwise have died, with a pig heart beating inside their chest.

Gentleman's clubs by definition are largely exclusive establishments. The members are mostly well-established, male (no female members allowed) and have pedigrees as long as your arm. Within the confines of the club, they are pampered and looked after on an almost individual basis.

Such a club exists at Thorney in Cambridgeshire and its facilities are second to none. All members are entitled to an individual room, each of which has a living and sleeping area, as well as en suite facilities. The chief steward is a man with the power to bar entry to all except those whose membership is deemed desirable and for the good of the organisation. It is he who is responsible for the efficient running of the establishment and he who maintains the high standard of the menu, which is prepared by trained nutritionists.

The premises have to be kept scrupulously clean and no one – staff or member – is allowed access without the chief steward's approval. All members have private health care, and medical treatment is available (if required) twenty-four hours a day, three hundred and sixty five days a year. All staff have to follow well drawn-up guidelines for the running of the club and any discrepancy in their behaviour which might cause embarrassment (or worse) for the organisation will result in dismissal from the job.

Exclusively a male environment, just two females are employed to look after the members in purely an administrative capacity. The members' bodily needs are almost entirely (apart from some meals) attended to by men. It is a very exclusive club.

The optimum number of members that can be accommodated at any one time is sixty-four (although there are expansion plans), and all are physically segregated at all times. They are within sight and sound of each other and can converse, but the management are very aware that fights might break out if they were allowed to intermingle.

The members are of course, if you had not already guessed, all pigs – pedigree pigs, from Landrace to Large White and volatile foreign Durocs. The club itself is an artificial insemination centre, where the animals are kept in strict isolation but in perfect comfort. In return they have to supply a sample of semen – usually no more than twice a week.

The boars are selected on their individual conformation and pedigree. They have to pass blood tests for Aujesky's disease, Brucellosis, Swine Fever and Blue Ear disease. In addition they also have to undergo treatment for Leptospirosis and skin tests for Tuberculosis. If all these tests prove to be negative, then the animals are eventually allowed entry (following a period of isolation) into the AI centre. The reason for such preferential treatment is to check the pig's breeding potential and high health status. Such qualities are much sought after by pig farmers wanting to introduce new, improved lines into their own breeding units without incurring the costs of buying a top class boar. Smallholders with even a very small numbers of sows find this service a particular value and often do not keep a boar on their premises at all.

The club's chief steward – otherwise known as the AI centre manager, Philip Rewse – trains the boars to perform to order. They come out of their pens one at a time and mount a dummy sow and produce the necessary sample. Some of the more reluctant boars have a spray of 'in season' sow from an aerosol can, which usually gets the required performance. The very shy sometimes in addition get a prostaglandin injection (not Viagra – although that might work just as well), which is very effective. The samples of sperm, once collected are moved to the laboratory, which is just next door to the boar's living quarters, through a simple double-hatch window. The sperm is checked for potency and processed before being dispatched the same day to inseminate, in the manner I have already described, sows all over England. The ejaculate from a boar is usually enough to impregnate about forty sows. Semen is also sent abroad to countries across Europe. A consignment went last week to Hungary for the first time.

Great care is taken to maintain the very high health status of the boars in the unit. All staff, vets – and that includes me as I visit twice a week – and any other visitors to the pigs, have to shower in and out and use clothing inside that never leaves the premises. All visitors have in addition to sign a declaration that they are pig clean (i.e. that they have not been near another pig for at least seventy two hours). Any visitors that cannot comply with this strict rule are not allowed into the building where the pigs are housed but can view any boar from the office, where there is a large inspection window overlooking a viewing pen.

Boars stay on the unit for about a year before they are moved on. Unlike their contemporaries in ordinary pig farms, who have to move to the abattoir when their breeding usefulness is finished, these privileged boars are (because of their value) usually sold on to work elsewhere for a time. It is then they will probably meet, for the first time since they left their mothers, a living, breathing, passionate female. Most AI centre boars rise to the new challenge and live on for a year or two more. But when their breeding days are finally over they too have to make their last journey to the slaughterhouse.

It's a sad end to a great life for a boar at stud, but given the choice I'm sure most male pigs would opt for it at birth. It's an old saying: 'Cats look down on you, dogs look up to you but pigs are equal.' Given the many examples of the parallel lives we lead, I'm sure most of you will agree.

CHAPTER 6

What a Dog!

MOST PEOPLE WHEN IT comes to animals, and to dogs in particular, fall into two distinct categories. There are those who love dogs and have kept them all their lives and there are others who say, and I hear it said so often, 'I would never harm one but' and leave the rest to the imagination.

Those of us in the first category would readily identify with Samuel Butler when he said 'the great pleasure of a dog is that you may make a fool of yourself with him and not only will he not scold you, he will make a fool of himself as well.' It's a good quotation and neatly sums up why so many of us love to keep dogs. In addition you can impart your innermost secrets, no matter how heinous, to your dog and it will still love you. It should come as no particular surprise that I admit to belonging to the dog loving fraternity and feel incomplete without a dog at my heel when I am walking, or at my feet when I'm sitting by the fireside. If you are going to keep a dog you should be prepared for it to be a large part of your life but there are limits. A dog will share in your thoughts, be happy with you and will know when you are angry, upset or in pain. A dog will know when to avoid you and when you need comfort. You are never alone when you have a dog by your side but still there must be limits.

You should never share your bed with a dog. Quite apart from the possibility that it might introduce fleas and other nasty creatures into your bed linen, it does give it ideas above its station in life.

A couple I knew shared their bed with a poodle every night. This dog ruled the roost day and night and had a very bad temper that was never checked. It slept between the husband and wife and if one of them turned over and touched the dog it would waken and bite the offender. The husband was a bit shame-faced when he told me but his wife was not in the least embarrassed. The poodle was her much beloved pet (child substitute) and whatever the dog wanted, he got. It was the ruination of what could have been, given the chance, a good dog.

A dog should never share in your food from the table. When you are eating, a begging dog is a pain in the neck and it will almost certainly be overweight due to this unhealthy practice. Sharing a sandwich while on top of a hill or whilst out fishing is however just permissible. Exceptions are all the better for proving the rule.

Dog lovers should not lose sight of the fact that there are many people who would rather not have anything to do with our four-legged friends. This second group of people would tend to agree with John Sparrow when he said they were 'indefatigable and unsavoury engines of pollution', and would wish along with Alan Bennett that they were a species destined for extinction. I can sympathise to some extent with the view, as most of us would having just trod in dog mess, but responsible dog owners everywhere should always try and ensure if their animal leaves a 'calling card' that it is cleared up before it annoys other people.

Most dogs, given the correct training, enjoy being well behaved and walking to heel. It can be very tempting in some circumstances to let them off the lead where there is no risk of them dashing out into the middle of a busy road or chasing sheep or other livestock. Some years ago I had a friend who had a very lively Labrador that, while not being vicious in any way, was still a bit of a menace. The owner did say that when she gave the command 'heel' in the approved Barbara Woodhouse voice, the dog was just as likely to grab the nearest one – just to be friendly – as obey the order, which gives you some idea of the owner's training skills. Matters came to a head one day during a walk along a riverbank. There was no one about and the owner thought it fairly safe to allow Paddy, the dog, off the leash. Paddy had a great time investigating under thorn bushes and paddling through boggy places where her owner was not inclined to accompany her.

The dog was in her usual excitable mode, dashing from one delectable smell to the next, when she spotted, around the bend of the river and down a rather steep banking, an angler. He was sitting in all innocence on a stool, concentrating on his rod and line and the bit of water in front of him.

It had been raining all day and Paddy, seeing this chap hunched under his umbrella, oblivious to the world, and being the friendly dog that she was, thought it would be nice to pay him a social call. Her dash down the slope, as she was incapable of doing anything slowly, became an uncontrolled slide. She hit the unsuspecting man full in the back and the fisherman, stool and various pieces of assorted fishing kit landed in the not too shallow or clean river. The dog followed him into the water and needless to say was first out as well. As the angler emerged from the river, dripping wet he was further insulted by Paddy shaking all the excess water from her coat all over him and then she proceeded to eat all the man's bait – including the maggots!

After this little episode my friend actually took Paddy to dog training classes but it didn't seem to make much of an impression. She never dared go back to that stretch of river again.

Among my many interests, which include golf and hill walking, is angling. I'm not keen on the sedentary sort of angling: on a bank, under an umbrella, waiting for mad Labradors to push you into the water. This type of fisherman sits for hours and puts all coarse fish caught in a net. At the end of the session, which can be all day, all the fish are returned to the river. I don't like this type of fishing. It is too inactive and while it may seem more humane than game fishing – the type I enjoy – it smacks to me too much of using animals as playthings. I am a hunter, a seeker after trout and salmon. Myself, my family and friends eat anything I catch, which most of the time is not a lot. I like to cook, as well.

Dogs as you might imagine – to return to the subject in question – are not very popular on many river banks and trout fisheries due to their potential for disruption and creating mayhem while their owner is concentrating on casting a fly over the water. This is a pity as a well-behaved dog enjoys a day out by a river just as much as his owner.

Some years ago I became a member of a fishing syndicate and part owner of a lake – in size about one hundred acres. It is a delightful, peaceful place teeming with all sorts of wild life. After a few expeditions on my own, I gave way to the imploring expressions of my two dogs and took them along with me.

Dogs, like people derive different pleasures from fishing. My retriever Saffron spent much of her time, apart from when she was sleeping, as she was by then quite old, in watching the birds and wild fowl. She seemed to be fascinated by the many different types of birds she studied. She was a canine 'twitcher!' We were in my small rowing boat one evening when even she was totally confounded. Over the top of us at about two hundred feet flew a creature that buzzed like a bee. It swooped overhead, disappeared, then came back and repeated the performance. It was like an ancient plesiosaurus and my old girl was absolutely amazed. Her eyes seemed to glaze over in astonishment and her jaw dropped open. She had never seen a powered hang-glider before. She wasn't frightened and the sighting made her evening. If it had been possible I'm sure she would have noted it down in her bird-spotting book. I can still see, even years afterwards the incredulous look on her face.

No such diversions would ever get the attention of my other dog; a Border Terrier called Tuppence (Tuppy for short). She was a consummate fisher who channelled all her terrier instincts into catching trout. Nothing and nobody and certainly not hang gliders could distract her from her abiding passion – the fish in the lake. She would spend all her time in the boat with her front feet on the gunwale eagerly scanning the water for any signs of trout activity. When a trout jumped out of the water, which was quite frequent, she would dash from one side of the boat to the other to enhance her view. This would make the boat rock from side to side but that never seemed to worry Tuppy. When a trout was stupid enough to take hold of my fly her enthusiasm was wild and her high-pitched scream of delight carried to all corners of the lake. The pleasure and excitement encased in that trembling small body as she watched the battle between the fish and the rod and line was a joy to behold. If I was a little slow in her opinion in bringing the fish to the side of the boat and into the net she was quite likely to jump into the water to lend a hand in catching it. I was then often faced with the dilemma of whether to net the dog or the fish first. I even on one occasion managed to get them both at the same time. Once the trout had been landed and duly dispatched, Tuppy would lose all interest in the captive and begin to scan the lake again, ever hopeful of more sport.

My current dog is an English Setter crossed with Labrador. She is called Tula Tika, which I was always told was a Zulu name meaning a 'peaceful wind.' Doubt was cast on this however by a South African vet who worked with me for a time. He said it sounded much more like the Khosa phrase, 'shut up' which was perhaps more appropriate for her when she was a young dog.

Tula enjoyed going fishing as well but never got into bird watching or trout mauling. She did however twice bring me injured birds that she had found in the bushes and deposited them gently in my hands. She would have made a wonderful gun-dog as she had a very soft gentle mouth, but had three major flaws in her make up. She was and is frightened of large noises such as thunder, fireworks and exploding guns. At the first sound of a gun firing she would be off into the middle distance of another field, which wasn't very helpful. She is also very lazy. She quite enjoyed picking up one bird on her own initiative but rapidly got bored and couldn't see the point of repeating the exercise. You could almost see the thought process: 'I can do that, but what's the point of doing it again?' Her third bar to being a good retriever was her aversion to water. She can swim but just doesn't like getting out of her depth. On two occasions I have gone for a swim with the dogs and both times Tuppy and Tula swam beside me, which was, I thought, rather sweet of them. Unfortunately however on both occasions Tula spoiled the effect by trying to climb on my back. Small children I can just about cope with on my back when I am swimming, but not large dogs.

Behaving well in public places is something as owners we all want our dogs to do. It gives a sense of well being and pride similar to that experienced when our children behave well when visiting a difficult relative. There are times as well when our dogs can put us to shame by behaving better in public than an owner.

A friend of mine acquired a new Labrador puppy called Cilla. When she was about nine months old, he took her to the lake to introduce her to fishing. She, like all Labradors, loved being outdoors and behaved impeccably. Soon they went out in his boat and she settled down happily at his feet on an old coat. After about two hours or so she became a bit restive and started pacing up and down and whimpering. Arthur thought she was just getting bored and told her to settle down but to no avail. The boat had been drifting nearer the banking and Cilla quite suddenly jumped out of the boat and swam to dry land. She then had a pee on the grass, jumped back into the water and swam back to the boat and asked to be taken on board again.

Not only had she obeyed all the natural rules of human convention and those of most water authorities by not polluting the water, she had also put her owner to shame. He readily admitted that she did more than he would have done in similar circumstances.

Some, probably most, dogs have great faith in their owners. They feel protected from harm and the world at large if they are with their 'pack leader.' Sometimes this faith can be eroded more than a little when the owner takes the dog to the vet's for treatment or an operation. Most animals, once they have first been through the surgery door, realise it is not an experience they wish to see repeated and will sulk for days after if an owner insists. There are, however, a few dogs that no matter what is done to them are always pleased to come to the surgery and positively welcome a visit.

Emma was a good example of this type of behaviour. She was a sweet-natured mongrel bitch who at first glance could have been taken for a retriever. She typified her owner (a local doctor) and family as many dogs do to perfection. Her nature was outgoing, generous and gregarious, with a slightly wilful bent for wandering off when the mood took her. It was this last flaw in her character – if such it was – which made a decision to have her spayed inevitable, before she became pregnant yet again by one of her many canine admirers in the district.

An ovariohysterectomy, although routine, is never especially easy when the patient is a trifle overweight and so it proved with Emma. The injection to induce anaesthesia, which is given into the vein, didn't work properly and the blood leaked from the vein into the surrounding tissues. The ovarian stumps were surrounded by fat and bled profusely and didn't seem as if they wanted to stop until the abdomen was entirely full of blood. Emma had to have a drip to help replace the blood loss and to cap it all her recovery from the anaesthetic was much protracted and accompanied by head banging and feet scraping. Because she had such a tough time we kept her in the clinic overnight just to keep an eye or her, to make sure she was going to be fit to go home the next day. When she did go home she was much bedraggled and a shadow of her old confident self.

However, she was back in the surgery just twenty four hours later, her inclination to wander not curbed in any way. She barged open the waiting room door and breezed in wagging her tail. Perhaps she was just stupid but I prefer to think she had a very forgiving nature and a faith that lightning never strikes twice. Whatever it was I always used to wish when days were long and hard due to difficult dogs that there were a few more around like Emma.

I have to admit at this point that I always have bitches. I will not have a dog. Dogs are distracted by matters sexual, are far more aggressive and, to my biased mind, are far less companionable. Having said this I know there are many good and faithful dogs on whom owners lavish love and affection, and that they are well rewarded in return. Perhaps my antipathy towards them was decided years ago by a friend's dog. Sam was a black Labrador from uncertain parentage, which under normal circumstances should almost have guaranteed a sensible dog with reasonable manners. Chris my friend took Sam on a pheasant shoot once and once only. It was quite a prestigious occasion with all the local farmers and landowners in attendance. All was well to begin with but when the guns started to fire Sam disappeared – up the back of his owner's Barber jacket. He put both front legs around Chris's waist and refused to let go or come out until all the banging had ceased. It was not as if he had never heard a gun fired before, he had – many times. But this somehow was different and his owner was present and ready to be hugely embarrassed.

Not that Chris was a stranger to ignominy when Sam was in attendance. Another of his less endearing little tricks was to pee down stationary trouser legs. It was never a good idea to stand still for too long when Sam was around.

It is very easy, living close in more or less happy harmony with a dog to attribute to it human characteristics and feelings. My children have always maintained that our family retriever Saffron, now long dead, was a sixties child. She was always free with her favours and very laid back. She could never be induced into doing anything she didn't want to do and did not have a vicious bone in her body. She was all for peace and having a good time. There is no doubt that all dogs, like most warm-blooded animals, experience pain, fear and hunger and remember all such occasions. I'm also sure that some dogs experience higher emotions such as love and jealousy, and will mourn the death of a canine friend or human owner.

I also knew a dog that did, I'm sure, suffer from an Oedipus complex. He was a champion Cocker Spaniel who was, on account of his good looks, in great demand as a stud dog. Unfortunately for his owner Norman, the dog was totally unreliable when it came to mating bitches. Sometimes he would, with great enthusiasm, and at other times would show no interest at all no matter how far an animal had travelled to be mated by him. I gave him hormone injections a few times to improve his libido but I was never really convinced they were very effective.

The reason behind his uncharacteristic behaviour became all too clear when his mother died. They had been living together for years, both in the kennels and laterally in the breeder's house and did not like being apart. It took a couple of weeks for him to get over his mother's death but after that he was never again fussy over mating. Young or old, black or golden, from then on he loved them all with total impartiality.

It can be quite easy, and mostly mistaken, for owners to believe that their dog is more intelligent than they first think. I remember vividly having a telephone conversation with a lady who was quite convinced that her dog was dying as he was digging its own grave before he expired.

The dog, called Hector, had been unwell all morning and was breathing very heavily. As the lady was speaking on the phone she described an old, very fat little Beagle dog furiously digging a large hole at the bottom of the garden. Would he get it deep enough before he conked out?

The owner was desperate for a house call to see if anything could be done for her dog before the Grim Reaper carried him off. I duly called round later to find that Hector was suffering nothing worse than a stomach upset. He was, like his owner, quite house-proud and was actually digging a hole into which he could vomit. An anti-vomit injection and some antibiotic worked wonders and he soon stopped 'digging his own grave.'

The tendency to impart human motives and thoughts to dogs mostly does no great harm and we all do it to some extent. If however a much-loved pet dies – or worse, disappears without trace – then owner and family can become extremely distressed. Dog stealing seems to be on the increase again and this may be the reason for the sudden loss of some animals.

One method to try and increase the odds of getting your dog back should it run off or get kidnapped is to have it microchipped. A very small chip about the size of a rice grain is inserted under the skin by the vet. This chip contains coded information, which will reveal the owner's name and address and telephone number. Any stray dog, or cat for that matter, will be scanned by rescue centres or veterinary practices as a matter of course and it then can be very easy to reunite owner and pet.

We have had many successes over the few years that this system has been running but it can provide unforeseen problems as well.

Quite recently a young German Shepherd dog was found running around a supermarket car park. It was taken to a rescue centre but for some unaccountable reason was not scanned for a microchip. One week later it was rehomed with a new family who proudly presented it to the surgery for vaccination. Parents and young children crammed into the consulting room and they were very thrilled with their new pet. Unfortunately for them when I checked the pup for a microchip, it was all too evident. The family was devastated and tears were shed. The surgery contacted the identi-chip company who quickly told us the name and address of the real owner. He lived two hundred miles away on the south coast and when we phoned him he did not even know that the animal was missing! It seemed the pup came from a broken home. Husband and wife had separated and the wife had taken the dog, and when she found it difficult to cope with she let it go to someone else, who had travelled to our area and promptly lost it in the Tesco car park.

The real owner wanted his dog back, but after a few hours of doom and gloom for the new family, he phoned me back. He had reconsidered his decision and if I could assure him that the dog would be well looked after he would leave it at the new home. I was very happy to do this. It was a successful ending to the saga, which before the advent of microchips would not have occurred.

It is a real dilemma for new owners of stray dogs, which have been with a family for some time. Only last week I ran the scanner over an old Labrador dog who had turned up at a farm over three years before. Yes, he had an old style chip inserted at least 5 years ago. The owner was distraught at the thought of losing her now much loved pet but I had to remind her that someone else might still be mourning its loss. I could not insist that we trace the dog back to where it came from – I am not allowed, for reasons of client confidentiality, to contact the identi-chip company about the dog. I had to leave it to the conscience of my client and as she left the surgery I was not at all sure she was going to do any such thing.

CHAPTER 7

A Farmer's Lot

FARMING HAS NEVER BEEN an easy way to make a living unless you happen to own a few thousand acres of fertile soil and have an easy market for the grain you grow. Livestock farming, as opposed to arable, has always been a more hazardous way of life, not least because the farmer's business is much more susceptible to factors which most of the time are almost totally out with anyone's control. Weather conditions, market prices and disease, while important to a crop only enterprise, is crucial to a farmer who looks to animals to make his living. It is sad but true the oft-quoted statement that, 'when you have livestock there will be times when you will have dead stock,' and there just isn't a stockman who has not experienced the gut wringing emotion of finding an unexpected death on the farm. It is even worse if the death could have been prevented.

The names of Foot and Mouth disease, Swine Fever and Fowl Pest still have the power to cause fear and dismay in the countryside and for good reasons. Very little can be done by an individual farmer to reduce the odds that his animals might be the next victims. There is of course Government compensation if a notifiable disease such as one of the above does strike a herd or a flock. But this rarely takes into account all the cost factors, the general disruption of rural life and the emotional distress caused by seeing your livelihood slaughtered and then burned to a fine ash on huge funeral pyres.

Farmers as a group of people are generally philosophical about things over which they have no control – they have to be. Unlike some small animal clients, they are not prone to hypochondria either in themselves – they are generally too busy – or for their animals. It's just too expensive to get the vet out for a trivial complaint. It's one of the drawbacks to be a being a vet in a rural practice. There are many occasions when an animal is sick or injured and could be cured but it is just too expensive to give it the treatment. Farming is a business just like any other and if the cure is not cost effective the animal will have to die. This does not mean it should or will be left to suffer. No vet would allow that to happen and those animals with no economic method of recovery will be euthanased in a humane manner.

Most farm calls are important. Some are to initiate and maintain herd health programmes and are vital to the health and well being of farm animals, as well as the economy on the farm. Many other farm calls are for emergencies where an animal has a life threatening condition and it is imperative that the vet responds to the farmer's plea for help just as soon as possible. I call it our 'fire brigade role' and I sometimes wish I had a blue light on the car roof to speed me on my way.

You never know when an emergency call is going to arrive. Last Thursday was a classic example. There was no hint of what was to come. I went out on a call to see a lame horse, leaving my colleagues to finish off afternoon surgery. Getting on for three o'clock the phone rang. It was a fairly standard request for assistance to a cow having difficulties in calving and the stockman wanted help as usual just as quickly as possible. One of my assistant vets, Simon, was dispatched to attend and I gathered from the measured tones over the radio-telephone that the situation was well under control.

Nothing more was heard for another half-hour, during which time I had attended to my patient, and was on my way home when the radio once again crackled into life. It was Simon wondering about my location as he could do with some help. I said I was on my way but what was the problem? Knowing this particular client and his cows I imagined that it would be the usual difficulty of not being able to catch the patient. I made a mental note to teach Simon how it was done and wondered if the metal can that was employed in the surgery car park to teach me was still there.

The answer when it came was a little different, and unusual to say the least.

Quote: 'We couldn't catch the cow but she ran into a building and we got her trapped in there but now she has jumped out of a window and she is stuck on a roof!'

I thought I wasn't hearing properly but when he was asked to repeat, the reply was the same again. I wasn't very far away from the farm; it only took about fifteen minutes to get there. I was directed to a small field next to the farm buildings and as I drove over the grass I could see over in the far corner a gathering of people.

They were grouped around a low wooden shed looking at a cow, which was partially perched on the shed's red tin roof. The animal's hindquarters were still stuck in the window of the adjoining building and she couldn't move any further. It was all too obvious how it had happened. I didn't really need to ask but I wasn't short of people willing to tell me how she got there. There were as many propositions as to the best course of action as there were interested spectators. With my arrival there was a sort of collective sigh of relief. Nothing was said but I knew they all looked to me to sort the mess out and it would be my fault if it all ended badly.

It was generally agreed that the patient had been a mite difficult to catch so it had been decided by the assembled company to entice her into the small building, which adjoined the poultry house with the red roof. The theory was that it would be, if she were so confined, much easier to get a halter onto her head. It was a good plan. She went into the shed without too much persuasion but before anyone could follow her inside to restrain her with the rope she had jumped through a very inviting open window. I imagine she was as surprised and shocked as everyone else was at being stuck on a roof, but she didn't look it. She gazed at us, prick eared, and with an expression that seemed to say; 'So what, not my problem – nothing to do with me!'

Where was Simon when all this was going on? Like all good vets he was round at the rear end of the beast, which as I have already explained was still stuck in the original building. He was, at the precise time of my arrival, delivering the cow of a very lively, lusty bull calf. Unfortunately however no sooner was the calf born than the cow's uterus prolapsed due to the pressure of the window ledge pushing up into the cow's abdomen.

My colleague with great presence of mind quickly organised the farmer's wife to bring a large clean sheet to support the protruding organ, and a bag of sugar. I took charge of the front end of the cow. It was time to finally get a halter on the beast and with this done some semblance of control was returned to the situation. We made a start in demolishing the chicken shed. It was a low, fairly dilapidated building and it didn't take long. Quite quickly the cow was standing with her front feet on the ground but still with her hind end in the original building. We all pulled on the cow's head and were able to pull her out of the window, as this needed to be done before we attempted to restore the uterus to its original position – out of sight – back in the abdomen. As her legs slipped through the window frame, she half fell to the ground, which fortunately was soft due to some overnight rain. You would have thought the animal would, having had a very traumatic experience, be finished being difficult, but you would be wrong. She immediately got to her feet and tried to run off again. Fortunately we had three men on the end of the halter to stop her and she did not get very far, but it did make life even more difficult for Simon, who was running behind her still trying to support the suspended uterus.

Finally she stopped running and the end of the halter was wrapped around a convenient post to stop any further escape attempts. The bag of sugar was produced and the contents were liberally sprinkled on the now engorged organ. It always seems a bit like magic to see the effect sugar has in reducing the size of living tissue. Sugar – or even better glucose if you can get it – shrinks the uterus by the osmotic action of the chemical on the tissues. Water simply poured out and the womb was soon back to something like its original size and was swiftly and easily replaced. Just to make sure it stayed where it should be, and in case the cow started to strain again, large stay sutures were put through the vulva, which would stay in place for two to three days. That done we all stood back, the cow was relieved of her tether and she staggered away, a bit wobbly on her hind legs, across the paddock without so much as a backward glance.

The only problem left to solve was what to do with the calf. The mother just at the moment was too traumatised to want to have anything to do with him. He had to be bottle fed that afternoon and evening. However, by morning, sanity had been restored. The cow had forgotten her roof-walking experience and was happily feeding both herself and her new baby son. Whether our client recovered quite so quickly was another matter and I suspect he will never forget the day his cow spent some part of the afternoon trying to give birth on a cold tin roof.

Farmers who find a cow with a prolapsed uterus always know that this constitutes a serious, life threatening emergency and will always want the vet to come out to the farm just as quickly as possible. Most of the time this is fine but just occasionally it can be difficult to respond straight away if another emergency is already demanding attention. This can be just as stressful for the vet as the client having to wait.

A call was received from a farmer who lived about fifteen miles from the practice premises. His cow had just calved a live calf (good!) but was still straining (bad!) and in the farmer's words was trying to 'push out her calf bed,' which means trying to prolapse the uterus. They were holding it in place but 'would someone come straight away?'

I had my hands inside a dog just at the time trying to stem the blood flow from an artery. There was no one else available and clearly I had to finish what I was doing before I could set out. This I did just as quickly as possible and rushed out of the surgery to the car to encounter the densest freezing fog. It took double the normal length of time to get to the farm and I eventually crawled into the farmer's yard about an hour and a half after the first call.

There was no one around to meet me but as I stood getting my bearings in the fog and shivering from the contrast between the warm car and the perishing cold, I could hear loud bellowing noises coming from one of the buildings. The racket seemed to be both bovine and human and appeared to emanate from a loose box just behind the hay barn. I gathered up my kit and rushed to investigate.

I looked over the half door and there lay a Friesian cow on her side with a large round-bodied youth lying on her neck trying to keep her head down. At her nether regions were two older men – the farmer and a helper – who were both lying at full arm's stretch pushing with all their might to hold the cow's womb in place. The men at the rear end were obviously completely whacked. Their faces were bright red with the colossal effort they were putting into stemming the flow of maternal material. Their hands and arms were smeared with bovine blood and excrement. They were desperate and had no more energy for shouting. This lack of noise was more than compensated for at the front end. Every time the cow moved, bellowed or tried to stand up she was told by her youthful attendant to 'lie down you silly old bugger!' He now seemed to have her skull in a headlock that would have made Mick McManus very proud. It was certainly effective at keeping her on the ground.

It only took a moment's pause at the scene to make me rush back to the car for some extra equipment. I quickly donned waterproof trousers and obstetrical gown, grabbed a needle and syringe along with some local anaesthetic and hurried back to my patient. With the minimum amount of preparation I knocked a needle into the inter-vertebral space at the base of the tail and injected about five millilitres of anaesthetic. It worked almost immediately. The cow stopped straining and bellowing as the sensation around her hindquarters was abolished. She relaxed and so did everyone else apart from me. I still had a job to do.

I lay down behind the patient and plunged my arms into the billowing masses of retained placenta and tried to find the uterus. It wasn't there. She wasn't prolapsed at all. It was quite secure and tightly held where it should be – inside the cow's abdomen. What the farmer and his assistant were trying to do was impossible. They were trying to push the placenta back inside the cow, thinking it was the uterus. The cow had only been attempting to do what nature intended; she was trying to complete the third stage of labour by expelling the now redundant afterbirth.

I lay there immensely relieved, as all I needed to do was give the patient just a little amount of help and remove the last vestiges of placenta that were still attached and then the man-made crisis would be over. I had only one problem. How was I going to explain to the farmer that he was a complete idiot and all their efforts and my call out had been a complete waste of my time and his money?

I admit in the end I did not tell the compete truth. I did say that the womb had not prolapsed but it might have done had they not acted as they did. If nothing else it spared their feelings and made the paying of my bill that bit easier. As for me it did feel a nice change to find an emergency that just for once wasn't.

Having a call out from the vet is to many a farmer's way of thinking an unnecessary expense. Many will go to any lengths to try and avoid having to call the vet with a request for a visit. Farmers and especially their stockmen will try and calf their cows when they are having obstetrical difficulties rather than making that costly (in their eyes) phone call. If the worst comes to the worst and they have to ask for assistance most will deny that there has been any delay or that they have already tried and failed to extract the calf. This can be really annoying for the vet as many times the visit will be too delayed and the calf already dead. This then makes the job much more difficult as a dead calf cannot assist with the birth process. In addition maternal fluids, which are vital to lubricate the normal birth process, will have dried up.

Most of the time the vet will suspect the farmer has been trying to calf the cow, but having no proof just has to grit his or her teeth and get on with the job in hand.

This has happened to me many times but one occasion was different. I was called out to a cow that had obviously been in labour for hours. The calf was dead – not only dead, it was dried out and beginning to smell. The cow was knackered and judging by the exhausted appearance of the many helpers they had been at it for many hard hours. They all to a man said that they had only just found the cow. They did try to give the calf a pull, they said, and when it wouldn't come out they stopped and phoned me. 'A likely tale,' I thought to myself, but donned my calving gown and said nothing more.

The normal position for a calf to be delivered is head first with the front feet on either side of the head, much like a swimmer ready to dive into water. The reason why this calf wouldn't be born was that one of the front legs was pointing backwards into the uterus. This was causing an obstruction at the shoulders. I scrubbed my hands clean then lavishly coated my hands and arms with lubricating fluid. As I approached the rear end of the beast I posed the question: 'Has anyone had a hand inside her?'

An emphatic 'no' and a shake of the head was the deadpan reply as I plunged my arm into the womb to try and locate the missing limb. With my fingers outstretched I could just about locate the end of the missing leg and foot. But there was something else. It was a hard, metal-like object, and round, and didn't seem to be anything to do with the calf. I grasped it in my hand and pulled it out. It was a wristwatch with a metal strap!

Faced with the evidence – it even had the farmer's name on the back – he had to confess it was his. They, the assembled company had been trying for over two hours to bring the backward leg forward as they had been very well aware why the cow had not been able to give birth in the normal way.

I managed with some difficulty to bring the leg forward and finally deliver the dead calf. If I had been called earlier, not only would the job have been much easier, there would have been a good chance the animal would have lived. There was also a very strong likelihood that the mother would contract an infection due to the less than antiseptic methods of the amateur midwife. As it was, the bill to the owner was going to be the same amount dead calf or not and he might just as well have called me at the right time. At least having a live calf and a less exhausted cow would have made the bill easier to pay.

Over the last few years cattle, and to a lesser extent sheep farmers have carried an extra burden with the diagnosis for the first time of BSE (Bovine Spongiform Encephalopathy in cattle) – better known as Mad Cow disease. A very similar condition called Scrapie exists in sheep but the existence of Scrapie has been known for many years. The problem with BSE being a new disease is that it was suspected to be the cause of the deadly brain condition in people, new variant CJD (Creutzfeldt Jacob Disease). The infective agent is a prion that results in some people (mercifully very few) dying due to non-reversible, progressive encephalopathy. This resulted in Government legislation, which stopped all cattle over thirty months old from being slaughtered for human consumption. The practical consequences were many but it required all adult cattle over that age to be slaughtered and their bodies disposed of very carefully. The farmer received compensation from the Government. Most of the time this was not a problem but an owner of three bullocks aged about three years old contacted me and explained the trouble he had.

All three animals had been grazing on Whittlesey Wash for over two years. He had originally intended sending them to the abattoir before they reached the thirty-month age limit. But he was unable to catch or restrain them in any way and had rather given up on them and left them to fend for themselves.

This went on for over a year until the bullocks started behaving like teenage delinquents, probably as grass was becoming scarce in their part of the fen. They would travel up to a mile from where they ought to have been and barge through fences and generally create mayhem. The crisis came to a head one night when they broke into a garden, trampled over flowerbeds and ate all the vegetables. Something had to be done and the farmer asked me for advice. He wanted me to dart the animals in order to catch them. This seemed a bit of waste of time to me as he was going to catch them in order to put them down and claim the Government compensation.

I suggested he cut out the middleman and find a marksman with a rifle who would do the job with a minimum of fuss, and it would be very welfare friendly. Doing it this way would be far less stressful for the animals than darting them and then transporting them to a knacker yard. Little did I realise what I had set in motion. The farmer thought he would be able to get someone who normally deals with deer. Riflemen regularly slaughter deer while they graze quietly in a field. They are dead before they hit the ground and strangely enough the sudden demise of one deer in a group with a single shot causes no upset to the others at all. Unfortunately he could find no one to do the job and eventually at my suggestion he contacted the local police firearm unit for help.

'Could they help'? he asked.

'Absolutely yes,' came the response. 'We will treat it as a training exercise at no cost to you.'

This was just what the beleaguered owner wanted to hear and it was so arranged. On the appointed day a small army of people turned out.

Eight policemen came in a large minibus. Six had high-powered guns, were dressed in camouflage gear and baseball caps. There were two officers commanding the unit. In addition to the farmer and assorted hangers-on there was myself, and an RSPCA officer who was there to see fair play. My role was to certify when the deed was done that the animals were dead and record their ear tag number for the benefit of the Ministry. Just to complete the gathering a police helicopter clattered overhead and was in radio contact with the officers on the ground.

The miscreants, blissfully unaware of their fate carried on grazing in their field just a few hundred yards away while the marksmen took up their positions. With the six men in place, crouched behind trees and under hedges, the senior officer checked with the helicopter that there was no one in range behind the cattle should any shots miss. 'All clear' was heard and the order was given to fire, and a fusillade of shots crackled across the fen.

Nothing happened! I expected all three bullocks to be dead on the ground but they without exception carried on grazing. There was a short stunned silence followed by some crisp words into the radio by the senior officer. After this came a veritable cascade of sound like machine gun fire from the guns. In the distance, two of the cattle slowly subsided with great dignity but the third, which had cunningly presented its backside to the firing-range, carried on eating as if nothing out of the ordinary had occurred.

It was stalemate. The police were reluctant to fire any more into an animal that clearly was not presenting its best feature for assault. This went on for quite a few minutes, as no one quite knew what to do next. Then the beast made a mistake. He probably was checking to see if his assailants had gone away. He turned his head and looked backwards and a single shot rang out. It was enough. The bullock keeled over. His happy, carefree lifestyle of eating and wandering wherever he and his companions chose to go was over.

I got into the farmer's Land Rover and drove over to where the bullocks lay, and checked that all signs of life had departed

They were all very dead. The farmer was pleased, as his problems had been resolved. The police marksmen I think were rather embarrassed that their initial efforts had been so unsuccessful. I made a metal note to check, if I ever again found myself in a similar situation, to make sure the sharp shooters knew to which part of the animal's anatomy it was best to direct their fire. I had unjustifiably assumed that they would know. At least the animals met their inevitable end with a minimum of fuss and without being involved in a stressful chase and capture. I just wish it had been less like a shoot out at the OK Corral.

A livestock farm is a dangerous place to live, work and bring up children. Not only do you risk falling into or under the maws of large tractors and implements, there is the clear and present risk of becoming infected by a disease, which can be transmitted from animals to man. While Mad Cow is a disease that clearly can infect people, there is very little risk to a livestock owner and his family from the disease. The same cannot be said for other infections such as Tuberculosis. Bovine TB is on the increase virtually all over the country after years of the infection being almost contained in the southwest of England. The problem now apparently is cows becoming infected by badgers who appear to carry the disease. Badgers are a protected species and can only be culled with Ministry approval and under special licence. Killing badgers around infected farms strangely enough however seems to make the problem in the long term worse rather than better. This is thought to be due to those animals that are not killed dispersing away from the area and taking the infection with them. In addition abandoned sets are quickly recolonised by new badgers that rapidly become infected themselves. I suspect that tuberculosis in farm cattle, with all the attendant risks to those who care for the beasts, will not be properly controlled until a good oral vaccine is available to control the disease in the badgers.

Lambing time is very special on most sheep farms. It is a time of high tension and very long working hours. It is a time when everybody would normally pitch in and help, but that must not happen. Abortion in ewes is an ever-present risk at this time of the year. The most likely cause of abortion in sheep is due to infection by an organism called Chlamydia and this can be very dangerous for women of childbearing age and young children. Young women, and of course pregnant mums, must have no contact whatsoever with ewes or lambs as infection can make a woman very ill and she would lose any child she might be carrying. Children as well should be kept well away from lambing pens as they too could become infected. Chlamydial infection causes severe flu like symptoms. Most sheep farmers will vaccinate a breeding flock against the disease, which will reduce the risks but not enough to allow female help in the lambing shed or field. The age-old tradition of bringing weak, cold lambs into the kitchen, which my father would do regularly to warm them up at the Aga cooker, is now realised to be much too dangerous.

Not all infections on the farm are life threatening but most are a nuisance. Ringworm is a case in point. On one of my farm visits, while I was at the kitchen table having a coffee the farmer's wife suddenly pulled up her T-shirt and exposed her abdomen. There, just under her tummy button was a perfectly round skin lesion. She wanted to know what it might be and I suspect she knew exactly what it was. It was a perfect example of Ringworm, which is a highly infectious fungal infection. I knew that the calves on the farm were covered in ringworm lesions. The lady herself had no contact with the animals and the only possible source of the infection was her husband. He was sitting at the table as well and she gave him a steely glare.

'You,' she said, 'are not coming anywhere near me until all the calves are treated and better.'

He had been putting off treating the animals because of expense. The infection does not harm cattle very much and is usually self-curing after two to three months. After his young wife's ultimatum, he was into the surgery next day to collect the necessary in-feed antibiotic.

Farmers are resilient; mostly very generous except when it comes to bill paying time and essentially quite cynical about the world around them. They tend to see through young vets who try to blind them with science to cover up their own deficiencies. I was all too aware of this one day when I leant over a very sick calf. It was, I thought dying from pneumonia. I was asked if I thought it would live and I unrealistically said that I thought it might as I was going to use a new wonder drug.

The reply was instant and to the point. 'Wonder drug? It won't be a wonder if it works, it will be a miracle.'

CHAPTER 8

A Camel with Attitude and Other Wild Animals

I HAVE ALWAYS HAD fairly mixed feelings about the use of animals as performers in circuses. I have never come across a circus animal, and I have seen quite a few in my time, that has been badly treated or neglected but it doesn't seem natural to train wild animals such as lions or tigers to do tricks. It is obviously very alien to their natures to perform in this way. I am also fairly sure that that the constant exposure to people and travelling around the country must be very stressful. To go behind the scenes and see the perpetual pacing up and down behind bars that big cats do for hours on end is not pleasant. To my way of thinking it must be an indication of deep distress, boredom or even chronic psychotic behaviour. I am very glad that, at least in this country, there does seem to be a move away from using wild animals that are in captivity in this way. Zookeepers and circus owners in this country are now much more aware of the needs of captive wild animals and are prepared to try and give them a more animal friendly and stimulating environment in which to live. How I wish it were more true abroad. One of the most depressing sights I have ever seen was about two years ago when I was in Thailand. Tourists were queuing to have their photograph taken beside a tiger, which not only was totally shackled so that it could not move, but had also been declawed.

Having said all that about truly wild animals I have to admit I have no objections at all to domesticated animals performing in the circus ring. Dogs, horses and even camels can be trained quite easily and many positively enjoy applause and having an audience.

It used to be quite common to get a call from circuses coming to the area asking if I would be prepared to look after any of the animal entourage in case of health problems. One such group was coming to Peterborough and the ringmaster gave me a ring when he was en route. I said 'yes' to the usual enquiry without giving the matter much thought. During these visits I seldom have to attend to anything more taxing than a cough or a minor sprain. However, this particular visit turned out to be rather different and one I would never forget.

The entire circus group was due to arrive on the twentieth of the month, which was a Monday. First thing that morning when I had hardly had time to draw breath, the boss of the circus phoned me with an unusual request.

'I've got a camel that needs to be castrated,' he said. 'Can you do the job?'

I gulped twice inaudibly and played for thinking time.

'How old is he?' I asked, hoping for something not more than two months old and weighing no more than a hundred pounds.

'He's about two years old and fully grown,' came the reply I did not want to hear. It seemed silly to ask whether the beast had one hump or two but I did. It was a two humped Bactrian or Asian camel. Given those unpalatable facts it seemed to be sensible – even prudent – to confess that I had not actually ever castrated a camel before.

The ringmaster was not put off easily.

'That's all right – no problem – really nothing to it. Have a word with my regular vet if you want any advice.'

The guy was in a hurry to get the job done. It seemed the camels were getting into the breeding or rutting season and the two-year-old male was getting rather smelly and difficult to handle. He concluded his plea by saying, 'the paying customers don't want to get too close to the camels when they stink so much and start spitting. When can you come?'

I have to say I was with the paying customers on that one, all right! Unfortunately I have this genetic weakness which makes it almost impossible to say no to a client however unreasonable the request and I agreed rather meekly to go along the next day.

Immediately after I got off the phone I ignored the mounting waiting list in the surgery and got onto the 'regular vet.' How did he castrate camels I wanted to know? The technique is not described in any of my surgical textbooks.

He was very helpful. 'Look,' he said 'forget it's a camel. Just treat it like a big sheep.'

Well that seemed to make everything very clear, I thought. But then I remembered that I had never seen a sheep that could bite, kick and spit all at the same time. Come to think of it I had never seen a sheep that could do any of these three things. I had to make one more phone call – to the Bayer Drug Company. I wanted to know the dosage for camels of a commonly used cow and sheep sedative called Rompun. Its effect when it works properly can be excellent but I wanted to know if there was any data for camels. There was but the advice did not fill me with confidence. The dose I was told was very variable – somewhere between fifteen millilitres and a whole bottle.

I spent a rather sleepless night worrying and morning came round all too soon. After morning surgery I packed my surgical kit and a lot more besides and headed towards Peterborough. My head was full of preconceived ideas of what I might encounter and different strategies I might have to use.

The camels were housed in a large, clean, roomy building, which, had I not known better, I might have believed to be purpose built for that species. It was ideal. The patient was called Joe and he was very large and hairy. He also looked very suspicious when I loaded a syringe and tried to get close to him. I managed with the help of the boss and assorted ring hands that were also jugglers, clowns and trapeze artists, to restrain Joe just enough to inject a carefully computed amount of the sedative into his neck muscles. He was not a happy camel but we succeeded after a bit of a struggle. We left Joe alone for ten to fifteen minutes and then went back to assess the effect of the sedative. He looked a bit sleepy but not sleepy enough. I decided to give him the rest of the bottle and we waited again. I fully expected him when I looked again to be on the ground, asleep – comatose. He was not. He was a bit unsteady on his legs and he yawned a bit but he was not about to give in easily.

Then I had a brain wave. 'As he is a highly trained circus animal,' I said, 'can't you order him to lie down?'

'Good idea,' said the boss, who up to that moment I could tell had been beginning to lose a little faith in me and was hankering after phoning his 'regular vet.'

He walked over to Joe, tapped him on the knee and shouted something, which sounded a bit like Arabic, in his ear. It worked. Joe obediently lay down.

As soon as he was off his feet we all rushed forward – me, ring hands and boss, and rolled him onto his side, where he lay without complaining. I injected local anaesthetic into the necessary parts and scrubbed up for the operation.

I gave the injection a few minutes to work and then, taking a deep breath and remembering the advice, 'it's only a big sheep,' got to work.

The operation lasted only a few minutes and was so straightforward it was a bit of an anti-climax. Within ten minutes the patient was sitting up and half an hour later, to my relief, was standing once again. He was a little stiff to be sure but he seemed to have survived the operation in better shape than the surgeon. I had put my back out while I was bending over the beast and it took me two days to recover. I won't forget Joe in a hurry, or he me. I rechecked him next day. His wound was a bit swollen but he was fine otherwise. He saw me coming across the yard and gave me look of pure malice and spat at my feet a large globule of stomach contents. I guess he wasn't in a hurry to give me a camel ride.

Although Joe was the first and, I suspect, the last camel I will castrate, he was not the first to be seen by me in the line of duty. My first was another Bactrian camel called Jenny, with a not unusual complaint. Her humps had fallen over. Humps are not, despite what some people believe, filled with water to allow the beast to travel over long distances in the desert without drinking. They are chiefly comprised of fat. This makes them the energy stores that the camel needs for long distance travel.

This particular animal's problem – she used to live at Edinburgh Zoo – was easy to diagnose. She was in poor condition after suckling a youngster and her fat store had become depleted – hence the falling over humps.

It took only a few weeks of extra feeding and a hefty worming dose before she was restored to her former glory.

Zoo animals are in general quite difficult to treat, as they are quite rightly not normally handled on a routine basis. Large cats such as tigers and lions have to be anaesthetised before they can be examined. Others such as monkeys can sometimes be examined without sedation but this can be fraught with danger for both the keeper and the vet. My first professional meeting with a monkey was a chimpanzee called Liza. She was not fully grown but was as temperamental as any teenager. She needed to be examined and the keeper spent fifteen minutes cuddling and bribing her before she would consent to be looked at.

She was in rather poor condition, with what perhaps might be a tooth abscess. She was also anaemic and had diarrhoea. We decided that, as she needed an injection for all three conditions, it was best to combine it all in one syringe as one dose. Bad tempered primates can be dangerous and are often enclosed in a crush cage before they are injected. Liza was quite small so we decided that as there were enough people to hold her we would do that instead, with one person to each limb while I gave the injection.

Liza was not pleased about being held. She was clever and knew something was in the offing. Her screams of outrage were to be heard all over the zoo, and that was just at holding her. When the injection was given the yells were even louder and the diarrhoea became more projectile and accurate.

Having given the treatment, we now had a dilemma, which the keeper should have explained before we embarked on the treatment.

When we let Liza go she would in all probability attack us as we left the pen.

A strategy was evolved. We carried Liza over to the cage door through which the vet, keeper and two helpers were hoping to escape unscathed. Then we threw her as gently as possible in a lazy loop as if she was flying through the jungle from one trailing tree branch to another over to the other side of the cage. There she did a perfect three point landing onto the top of a bench.

As soon as she landed she turned, bared her teeth, screamed and came hurtling towards us with malicious intent as we tried to scramble out of the door.

We all made it out safely enough but it was a close call. My discomfort at the situation was not improved by realising, as we reached the safety outside the cage, that we had been watched by an ever increasing audience who were most amused. The little lad in the front row of spectators summed up the whole situation very neatly with his question:

'What's the vet doing mum?

There was no easy answer.

Not all the wild animals we treat are kept in circuses, zoos or wildlife parks. Many private owners keep exotic animals such as snakes, monkeys and spiders. They bring them to the surgery where sometimes they pose handling problems. Snakes are usually carried enclosed in large bags and when they are allowed out – if they are Boa Constrictors or Pythons – they will often coil themselves around the consulting table and refuse to let go. To give medication to such creatures is not without some inherent difficulties as it is not easy to give repeat injections, or dose with tablets if they refuse to eat. One such case a month ago required medicating by stomach tube daily for a few days. It was not easy but it was manageable. How we would have managed if the snake had been venomous I do not know.

Ornamental fish such as Koi carp often come to the surgery in large water containers or, if the fish is not so big, in water-filled polythene bags. The common cause for seeing them is either skin ulcers or abscesses. The most frequently used treatments for these types of condition in large fish are antibiotic injections. Fish don't enjoy being injected very much but it can be done, although the vet or nurse often gets soaked for their trouble. Fish do also get cancer and while the prognosis for treatment is usually not good, many owners will opt for surgery if they are sentimentally attached to their pet (not very likely, being a fish) or (more likely) the fish is a very valuable specimen and would be costly to replace. Operating on fish poses its own difficulties but they can be anaesthetised long enough to allow them to be removed from the water for the operation. The anaesthetic is dissolved in a special bath of water into which the fish is introduced. After a few minutes the fish is unconscious and can be removed onto a wet towel to keep the animal moist while the operation is carried out. The recovery from the anaesthetic is usually very swift following reintroduction into its normal environment.

Many of the wild animals that we see and treat are indigenous to this country. All vets in practice, whether they work in towns, cities or in the country, will see birds with injuries and fledglings that are commonly found under hedges or trees by enthusiastic, caring children. We always try to impress on children when they find a young bird to leave it alone. The youngster's parents were probably watching and waiting to feed it. Bringing it to the surgery will mean it will have to be hand reared, which is never easy. It also then becomes almost impossible to return it to the wild if it ever manages to grow to maturity.

One group of wild animals that are very common and very rewarding to treat is hedgehogs. Hedgehogs are walking repositories for ticks, lice and fleas and when one comes into the surgery, whatever the animal's initial complaint, we rid it of its pests. Hedgehogs can get by very well without them.

Most hedgehogs are brought to us by gardeners and the most

common complaints are broken legs and lacerations. These are treated in a very similar way to any other small animal. The only difficulty is to get the creature to unroll every time it needs to be looked at. The spines are there to protect it and they certainly do just that most of the time. Every vet or nurse has his or her own method to get the animal to relax and open up. My preferred way is just to stroke the spines from head to tail and this usually works in a few minutes. Many hogs, as we tend to call them in the surgery, after they have been confined for some time become totally relaxed in their surroundings and with the people who are looking after them. They then don't feel under threat and may not feel the need to roll up and protect themselves at all.

Last year we had a hog brought to us that was no problem to unroll. It was completely bald. It had no spines at all. A client had seen him in her garden, felt sorry for him and brought him into the surgery for treatment. He was the success story of the year, which had nothing at all to do with me. Indeed I knew nothing about him until he was well on the mend.

He had Ringworm, which is caused by a fungal infection of the type that affects dogs and cats. The lesions fluoresced under ultra violet light, allowing the diagnosis to be made. The treatment was very simple. He had to have a dose of griseofulvin in his food daily. This is an antibiotic, which specifically acts against the fungal infection and kills the spores. He ate his medicated feed willingly, which was not surprising as it was a most superior type of cat food. The griseofulvin was the powdered variety, which is normally used for treating cattle.

He was in a cat cage in the isolation unit for about two months, during which time his spines grew back to all their former glory. He was no trouble at all to handle as he came to trust the nurses and seemed to enjoy being fussed over. My only concern was that he might not rehabilitate in his garden and that the owner of the garden from where he came might not recognise him and think we had switched him for another.

However, all was well and he went back to the garden. Like all hedgehogs he had no problems getting back to his old lifestyle and was soon flea-ridden again. I also understand he never lost his taste for cat food and would turn up every night without fail for a saucerful.

If you have hedgehogs in your garden you will do them no harm at all by feeding them cat or dog food occasionally. This may in many cases help the weaker members of the species more easily survive the winter. They in turn will repay you by eating many of your garden pests such as slugs and snails but they might also infest your dog and cat with their fleas and ticks. Two words of warning however. Never give a hedgehog milk as this can cause perpetual diarrhoea; and do not use a dog or cat flea product on the animal without checking with your vet first that it is suitable to use. Some flea preparations are poisonous to hedgehogs.

The other native wild animal we commonly see and sometimes treat is the fox. It is unusual to treat a wild adult fox that has been injured by a car or by gun or trap. It is far more humane to put them out of their misery quickly and easily by injection. However, I do see and treat quite a lot of foxes; these are usually 'rescued' as very small cubs, dug out of dens with their mothers. The vixen is killed as a pest and then no one has the heart to kill the youngsters. I don't like seeing really wild animals such as foxes in captivity, as even those reared by hand from a very early age never really lose their fear of people and have a dreadfully restricted existence. I knew of one pair of foxes – a dog and a vixen that were reared together from an early age. It was fun watching them happily frolic around the pen but it didn't last. The dog had to be castrated when it neared maturity for obvious reasons. One cold windy night a wild fox came along when the vixen was in season and dug her out of the compound, leaving her castrated friend behind. The dog remained in captivity for about eighteen months after this but was visited occasionally by the liberated vixen. She would call at nighttime when it was all quiet.

He died quite suddenly without showing any clinical signs of illness, and while I hesitate to be emotive about the subject, I think he just lost the will to live.

He had looked a very miserable, lonely creature and everyone who looked at him felt sorry for him, but it would have been impossible to release him into what would have been to him a hostile environment. Better by far if he had been killed with his mother rather than undergo the torture of captivity and the loss of littermate and friend.

Not all fox cubs are lonely in captivity. There is one I know, reared by the same lady (Anne) who had looked after the two littermates, that is still alive after twelve years. He lives with a Malamute. This is a large Husky-like type of dog, and the two seem to be the best of friends. The fox however will only eat when Anne feeds it and if she is away for any reason it will take the food and hide it and will only eat when she returns.

The one fox that seemed to positively enjoy captivity was called Winky Woo. He was a castrated dog fox. He too had been obtained as a very small cub and his owners had put a great deal of thought, time and money into making an environment in which he seemed entirely happy. He had a large, safe, outside run from which escape was impossible, with lots of toys with which he seemed to enjoy playing. There was a series of large cat flaps, which allowed him access into the lower part of the house. He played with the family Labrador and two cats.

All was well for many years, then he seemed to have a problem with his mouth. It wasn't possible to look into his mouth properly without sedation – he wasn't that tame – and when I did this I found he had a cancerous growth on his gum. The owner insisted that the cancer be removed, which I did, and he then had radiation therapy at a treatment centre near Newmarket. This stopped the cancer from recurring and spreading for some months but the end was inevitable, as with all tumours of the mouth. It did grow again and he had to be put down. To this day I'm not happy that I was right to allow the fox to be subjected to this treatment as I was never sure whether it was concealing the pain and distress signals that I would have picked up from most dogs. But I do know he seemed to be quite happy during the extra few months' grace that the radiation treatment gave him. His owner was pleased that he had been given the very best of treatment despite the cost involved, which was considerable.

Some wild animals positively revel in captivity. I am still amused by recalling a friend's dilemma of a few years ago. He phoned me one evening to ask my opinion about a small furry creature he had rescued from the middle of the road. It happened in town one summer evening; instead of swerving around the creature, Les stopped and, as it was very quiet, he picked it up and took it home. He then persuaded it into a cage where it stayed for a few days, happily eating all sorts of goodies.

After a time, Les began to worry about the true identity of the creature and at my suggestion brought it to the surgery for identification. I had a rather furtive meeting with him and the encaged animal in the surgery car park, as he seemed reluctant to bring it into the building. The furry animal in question was a very large, brown common rat! It was sitting up in the cage and chewing on a delicacy. Les had begun to suspect the truth and was now very embarrassed at this revelation and asked what he should do with the creature.

As a farmer's son, I'm no lover of vermin and told him what he should do, but I knew from the look on his face that he wouldn't. He had grown quite attached to it having fed and looked after it for a few days.

I saw Les again a few days later and he told me he had taken it down a country lane and opened the cage door and let it go. It had scurried off in true rat fashion without so much a grateful backward glance or even a 'see you later sucker!'

The rat had obviously been restored to full health by Les's careful nursing and may well have been quiet initially as the result of unsuccessful poisoning. I'm sure given the choice it would have stayed in the cage quite happily for as long as Les was pleased to feed it and look after it. Rats are often the exception to normal wildlife rules.

CHAPTER 9

Birds of a Feather

IN MY EARLY YEARS in the practice I was occupied quite heavily in poultry diagnostic work. This was due to Silcocks, a large supplier of animal feeds, having an office in the town. The reality of what this entailed was less than glamorous. It meant that when all the major poultry diagnostic laboratories were closed for the weekend we, the practice, being open and willing got the work. It was not uncommon to have a large sack full of dead hens delivered on a Saturday afternoon. The job then was to post mortem all the dead hens to try and diagnose the cause of their demise. The duty vet had to do this and still fit in all the other routine emergency surgery jobs and visits that invariably tended to happen on a Saturday afternoon. There was only one thing worse than doing the job on a Saturday and that was doing it on a Sunday if there wasn't time the previous day (live patients came first). The smell was worse!

The essential requisite for the job was not a knowledge of poultry pathology but an enquiring mind and a strong stomach. As far as the smell was concerned I always found that a pipe full of strong tobacco – lit and drawing well – helped considerably to lessen the impact. My partners and colleagues relied on Players Senior Service cigarettes. The duty nurse always avoided the post mortem room and my then wife told me to keep well clear until I had showered and changed. Almost everybody, after the Silcocks organisation left town and the routine post mortem work ceased, gave up smoking! Somehow we just didn't seem to need tobacco any more.

A few months before this type of work stopped I had a life enhancing experience as the result of the poultry work. I had never been too keen on hens. This was the result of having, as a young lad, to clean out hen huts and collect eggs in nest boxes that might harbour the occasional rat. Henry the hen changed all my negative feelings towards chickens.

Henry was, in her way, a very ordinary hybrid hen. She came to the surgery with a batch of chickens for post mortem. There were four dead, two dying and Henry. I processed the four dead hens and euthanased the dying and did them as well. As my hand stretched out for Henry (Henrietta the Hybrid to give her full title) she played her trump card. She looked me very firmly in the eye and laid an egg. I was pretty sick of the whole business anyway but after a vir-tuoso performance like that I would have defied anyone to do other than pick her up and take her home.

At this time of my life I had two small daughters, one of whom was keen on ponies and the other on cats. The result of this was we had a large straw-filled stable containing a pony and various cats. I was reasonably sure that Henry would be all right with the pony but not so sure about the cats, but I was willing to take a risk. I ensconced the very bedraggled, feather-damaged little red chicken in a corner of the building where I kept a small store of hay, and hoped for the best.

Apart from worrying about the cats perhaps seeing her as a plaything or supper, I was concerned whether a battery bird would be able to adapt to a farmyard (or in this case a backyard) life. She had after all been debeaked and spent her first few months of exis-tence in a metal cage, crammed together with at least six others of her kind. The space in any battery cage is very limited and there is no room to stretch, flap wings or behave in any way like a normal chicken in a normal country or free range setting. In addition most battery hens are debeaked and Henry was no exception, which means the top half of her beak had been removed by a cautery machine. This is to stop feather pecking and cannibalism, which is a very com-mon problem with battery hens that are closely packed together. Many birds also have brittle bones due to the confinement and lack of exercise and legs can be broken very easily.

I need not have worried. Within a matter of a few days she had settled in remarkably well. Her feathers grew back very quickly and she soon looked magnificent. Her greatest pleasure was to take a dust bath in one of the rose bed borders. It's a common sight to see free range hens luxuriating in dusty soil. She couldn't have seen any other hens behaving like this and copied them; the instinct for the behaviour must have been in her genes.

Her assimilation into the way of life in the backyard, garden and orchard was complete when I noticed the cats (three in number) allowing her to groom them while they slept. She would comb through their hair with what was left of her twisted, distorted beak. I presume she was looking for something edible. She was a portable bug hunter and cleaner and although the cats could never be quite free of fleas, I'm sure her ministrations must have reduced their total flea population by quite an amount.

She would spend many nights roosting on the pony's back, which made grooming the animal a bit of a nightmare for Carol, my eldest daughter. The dogs mostly ignored her. When she was angry or frightened her habit was to leap into the air and emit a large squawk that was enough to unnerve any possible enemy.

Within a matter of weeks she had established a routine, which varied only with the weather conditions. If it was very inclement she would stay in the stable and lay her daily egg. If it was fine she would be off fairly early – around seven a.m. in the summer months. Her first port of call was through a neighbour's garden to another cottage where she would peck on the French windows and be rewarded with crumbs of toast. I was told she preferred the bits with marmalade. The morning egg would then be laid elsewhere – under the hawthorn hedge or round the back of the summer house were just a couple of her favourite places. She certainly kept the children looking and guessing.

Come the afternoon, she was usually back in the yard or garden scratching for worms in the compost heap or grooming the cats, and she would then wait for her dish of layer crumbs on the back door step.

She went missing once when another neighbour locked her in a shed as she had been picking the hearts out of his young vegetables just as they began to grow well. She returned from her prison after a couple of weeks looking almost as bad as when I first brought her home. I thought a fox had claimed her but she was soon restored to rude good health and was just as incorrigible as ever.

She lived with us for about four years all together, which is quite a good life span for a hen. I eventually had to put her to sleep when she developed ovarian tumours. She is buried along with all the other dead pets in the garden at the back of the house, and she gave me as much pleasure watching her behaviour as any of them. She also gave me cause to think many times of the distress we all cause to so many battery hens. Henry was no different to any of them apart from being a lot healthier. They all have the potential to enjoy their short lives in a similar way to Henry if only they had the opportunity. We could all help, in a small way, more hens to enjoy a happier existence if we insisted on buying only free-range eggs. I know they do cost a bit more but millions of battery hens would benefit.

As you will have now realised, I am not very keen on birds of any description being kept in cages. It doesn't matter whether it is hens being kept for egg production or small birds such as budgies or their larger cousins parrots, they should all be allowed out from close con-finement for at least part of the day. Whether you can easily get them to return to the confines of the cage afterwards is another matter. It is either cage and let them out or keep them in an aviary where they can fly around all the time if they should so wish. Even parrots like to fly around a bit given the chance and if you do have birds and you can't allow this to happen you should perhaps reconsider whether you should be keeping one in the first place.

I do have to admit that some small birds can be perfect pests when you do let them out of the cage. A friend who had a budgie let it have free range in the living and dining room. During dinner parties it was apt to fly down onto the plate and help stir the gravy for you with its feet. This particular bird died a year or two ago and I think despite the pain involved to the owner at the time met a near perfect death.

Its habit when the owner was working (she is a writer) was to sit on her shoulder, while she sat typing. It would nibble her ear and mutter little terms of endearment, or was it encouragement, at the same time. One day while on its usual perch it suffered what I presume was a heart attack – in mid sentence – and fell from its perch in a graceful parabola. It was dead before it hit the carpet. It was a fitting finale. The owner was distraught but the owner's friends were relieved. No more feathers in the soup!

Budgies I do find quite fascinating. They are friendly, happy little birds, not aloof like canaries or finches, and are such good fun to have around the place. They are really good pets for older people who may be a bit frail and not physically up to having a dog or a cat. As a child my younger sister was allowed to keep two budgies in a cage in the farm kitchen. They were male and female and the traditional colour for budgies – green.

They were a devoted pair and the female was always laying eggs. It must have been a very frustrating time for her. A friend who knew a thing or two about keeping budgies suggested that we attach a nesting box to the side of the cage and see what happened. My sister was warned not to expect too much as he had added that he thought the kitchen was too noisy and busy to allow the birds enough peace and quiet to incubate the eggs, but he thought it was worth a try. He had not reckoned on the persistence and determination of our loving pair of birds.

About three weeks after the nest box was attached there was a terrific commotion in the box. It was party time for the budgies! An egg, one of three, had hatched out. The baby looked ridiculous. It was, in the manner of all new-born budgies, blind and bald. It looked like ET on a bad day. But the proud parents were ecstatically happy. It was as if they had consumed a bottle of champagne each.

They were both very good about feeding the youngster regurgitated seed from their crops, and they both took turns at feeding, but they did quite forget to incubate the other two eggs. The result was the second egg was 'stillborn' and refused to hatch. Fortunately the warmth generated by the first baby incubated the third egg and it hatched out a week later. The mum and dad had another party and the excitement knew no bounds. As the offspring grew it was soon apparent that they were going to be a different colour to the parents. Two green budgies had given birth to two blue budgies. They did produce more babies over the next few years but nothing quite matched the excitement of the first occasion and they always produced blue youngsters.

Budgies are usually talkative little birds and seem to be able to chatter away quite coherently to their owners. The owners in turn tell me what they are saying but they might just as well be talking in Swahili as far as I am concerned as I can never understand a word. Usually the owner has to translate every utterance before I get the gist of what is said and it's not usually worth waiting for when it does come. If you are waiting for a sick budgie to give you a list of its symptoms then forget it! However you might, if you are lucky, get some help from the owner. But don't bank on that either. Some years ago now I was called to an old lady's house in Chatteris to see her budgie, which was reported as being very sick. The bird was huddled in the corner of the cage. Her feathers were fluffed up and she had been vomiting the contents of her crop.

It's not easy to give a small bird a full clinical examination but as far as I could tell there were no obvious signs as to why it was so sick. I asked the lady for a little history and then all was revealed.

Most evenings the bird, being a bumptious little budgie, was in the habit of sitting on her owner's shoulder, chirping in her ear and accepting a small piece of whatever the lady was eating or drinking. The previous night it happened to be a gin and tonic they were sharing. The budgie had a sip too many and was paying the price of over indulgence with a hangover! The cure was a little extra warmth and a blanket over the cage for a few hours to cut out the light and increase the temperature in the cage. It was restored to its usual prattling good health by the next morning.

Keeping budgies and parrots can be very rewarding but it does have its dangers as well. These birds can be carriers of a disease called Psitticosis. The infective agent is a Rickettsia type of organism, which is halfway between a virus and a bacterium. The disease can kill a bird but it can be very dangerous to people as well. It can cause severe flu like symptoms, pneumonia and sometimes death if untreated. I am always very suspicious if a bird or an owner is unwell and the bird is a fairly new acquisition.

It was commonplace until a few years ago to have large numbers of parrots and other psittacine birds imported into the United Kingdom. They arrived from all over the world but mostly from South America and Africa. Very many of these birds carried the disease when they arrived into this country as well as many other exotic infections. Most of these birds were netted in the tropical rainforest and were imported to this country to satisfy the demand from the pet trade. Very many died in quarantine and it's a business I'm so glad has been brought to an end by Government restrictions. I used to look after a number of these quarantine centres, where the birds were kept for months before they were released and allowed to be sold. I always wore a mask when I went into a quarantine station to try and make sure I did not contract psittacosis. One quarantine owner used to scoff at my precautions and never bothered for himself. He contracted the disease, was very ill and nearly died. He gave up the business after he recovered.

Psittacosis is now much more rare as all birds for the pet market are hatched and reared in this country. It's more humane and safer for everyone concerned. But it is still a disease to look out for if you have recently acquired a new bird and it becomes ill with diarrhoea, ruffled feathers and laboured breathing.

The average parrot, whether it is an African Grey or an Amazon, can be a wonderful companion and mimic, but can also be dirty in its personal habits and difficult to look after. Parrots can become stressed and upset very easily. It's not difficult to see why, considering most of them are kept in cages on their own and without contact with any other parrots. My first ever encounter with a stressed parrot happened one evening on a night of freezing fog. I had to travel a round trip of about twenty-four miles to see a bird whose owner thought it was extremely ill. It was ill, mentally ill – in fact a neurotic wreck! It was completely bald from the neck down and was scampering around its cage like an overactive John Cleese. At the first sign of a feather emerging from one of its follicles, it would emit a screech of demented pleasure and pluck it out.

Polly was not very informative as to what was going on but after a fairly detailed examination of the skin, I didn't think the problem was physical. There was no evidence of infection, infestation or hormonal imbalance.

The bird was bored out of its brain being confined to a small cage all the time, with only humans for company. And it certainly got attention being a bald, feather-picking bird, but not the sort of company and companionship it needed.

On my recommendation it was sent to an aviary from where it was purchased with lots of other birds of its own kind and within three weeks its feathers had grown back well and it was a happy, well-adjusted bird again.

Having established that some birds can seriously damage your health from infection, there are other, much larger that can be quite dangerous to handle. Ostrich farming came to the Fens a few years ago. Mature birds stand up to eight feet tall and need specialist housing and enclosures. Big as they undoubtedly are, they were at the end of the queue when the Almighty was handling out the brains. They are genuinely very stupid birds and can be quite aggressive, especially in the breeding season. They can kick in a very vicious way that has been known to kill. What has to be remembered by everyone who handles them is that unlike every other species I know, ostriches kick forwards, not backwards. Fortunately, as they are so stupid, once they are caught by the neck, and the head lowered to near the ground, a sock or some similarly 'high tech' piece of equipment placed over the head will render them immediately and completely docile. But I still don't trust them not to kick and keep well out of the way of any potentially flying feet.

The costs of setting up an ostrich farm can be very high, not only because of the specialist equipment, such as fencing and buildings, which is required but also the initial cost of buying breeding birds. One farmer I know spent eleven thousand pounds on importing a breeding pair from South Africa. Fifteen years ago this was expensive but the economics of doing it then seemed to be sound. Ostriches can have a breeding life of about forty years and can produce up to sixty eggs in a breeding season. Each egg then was worth, if it was fertile, about one hundred pounds and young chicks after a few weeks of age were worth over one thousand pounds each. At the time it all seemed to be too good to be missed and ostrich farming seemed assured of a bright future in Britain.

The numbers of the birds increased dramatically for a few months, as many farmers seemed to see a bright future and good profits and jumped on the bandwagon. This was followed by a slump and the cost of non-breeding animals fell drastically. This was good from the consumer's point of view as meat from the birds is very healthy due to the low fat content, and for a time in Britain it was hoped that they would become the new 'beef on two legs' However, the boom did not happen. Quite a few farmers lost a lot of money. There were problems with finding suitable abattoirs to deal with the birds in a manner that was suitably welfare friendly. There was even prolonged discussion and disagreement as to the best method of slaughtering the birds. South African methods were deemed (rightly!) by our authorities to be unacceptable in the UK. Birds owned by a client in Cambridgeshire had to be transported to Aberdeen-shire before they could be killed for the table.

It was all very unsatisfactory but the main reason ostrich farming did not become the saviour of livestock farming in England – despite the healthy meat and a skin and feathers that can be very valuable – was that the British public were not prepared to demand ostrich meat from the supermarket or ostrich burgers from the fast food outlets. There are still a few ostriches around the countryside, but I for one am not too sorry that I no longer have to look after their health requirements.

Like most vets in practice I find the diagnosis and treatment of birds, especially small caged birds, difficult and demanding. Too often the cause of an illness is only discovered at post mortem. Handling a small bird that is unwell causes a lot of stress and is often enough to cause it terminal decline as a result of shock. Too many vets have had the mortifying experience of holding a bird – even to clip its nails – only to have it die in their hands. It is often best to observe it through the bars of the cage and make a tentative diagnosis at a distance. Medication is usually a matter of putting antibiotic in the drinking water or feeding specially medicated seed.

A sick bird needs subdued light and a warm atmosphere. In the winter months this is fine during the day when the central heating is switched on, but many owners forget that the bird could get very cold through the night when the heating is off. During the summer it can be easy to 'oven cook' a bird by leaving a cage near a window, with no ventilation and without shade on a hot, sunny day. Even a bird bred for the tropics can find it very hard to cope with these types of conditions.

Even observing small birds from a distance can be traumatic. A vet friend still remembers with anguish peering through cage bars at a little bird that was lying on its side in one corner. He had been told the bird was a 'little off colour.' He turned to the owner – an elderly gentleman and said, 'I'm terribly sorry but I'm afraid your little Jamie has rigor mortis.'

'Oh dear,' came the reply, 'is that very serious?'

He vowed after that to make his explanations a little less technical!

CHAPTER 10

'I Know Two Things About a Horse and One of Them is Rather Coarse'

I DON'T LOSE MY temper very often – in fact hardy ever – but I have been known to 'lose it' when I attend to an animal, and it is often a horse, that has been caused much pain and suffering through ignorance or thoughtlessness by an owner. Many horse owners will profess to be very knowledgeable with regard to their animals, and some are, but a greater majority are not – but that does not stop them imparting an 'expert opinion' to other equestrian owners, often to the detriment of the horses in question. I find it especially galling, as horses are my favourite species to treat as they pose very different problems to other large animals such as cattle. Farm animals are all sentient creatures and experience pain, anger and fear but horses in a unique way somehow have the ability to inspire great affection, even love in the people who care for them. Many horses have a sheer physical presence, beauty and grace in movement that can be recognised by even those people that would not tell a hock from a dock.

Our attraction to them may be something to do with the eyes. The equine eye has the largest ball of all the land animals, with eyesight that can be as effective in the darkest conditions as in daylight. This is because its retina magnifies objects fifty percent more than the human eye. The horse's sense of smell is even more acute than its vision. The awareness of different smells has evolved like its sight over millions of years to help the animal escape from predators. Horses now still put it to good use to always recognise people they like and to be fearful of those they don't trust – like vets. And they can distinguish between male and female vets!

We may admire them most of all for their amazing physical

attributes. Their strength, speed and stamina are outstanding and are without equal. Endurance rides, where an animal will take its rider fifty to sixty miles in a day, in safety and without harm to itself or its companion, are in my opinion even more admirable than show-jumping or racing. Endurance rides are closely monitored by equine veterinary surgeons, who have the power to stop any horse and rider from going on if it is felt there is a risk to the animal's health.

Which brings me to remember one occasion during an endurance ride where I was a veterinary supervisor, and much younger. I was examining a horse at a checkpoint and said to the rider that I was rather concerned that the animal was sweating a bit more than I thought it ought to be. The lady was rather heavier than she should have been, given the nature of the event and size of her horse, and drew herself up to full height and majesty.

'Young man,' she said – I was then – 'If you had been between my legs and working as hard as my horse for the last two hours, you would be sweating as well!'

There was no ready made answer to this rebuff but I still gave her and her steed a period of compulsory rest until they were allowed to ride on.

Tetanus, or 'Lock Jaw', has been known about and recognised by vets and horse owners for a very long time. It is a horrific illness that causes the animal that is unfortunate enough to contract it to suffer very badly before it dies. It is caused by a small bacterium, which is present in the soil. There are treatments available to help the animal attempt to recover but most of the time these are even today unsuccessful. The awful irony of the disease is that it is so easily prevented with a small dose of vaccine, which is relatively cheap to buy. What are a few pounds, and it is just a few, against the life of a horse?

I can so easily bring to mind my first case of clinical tetanus. It took no thought or test to diagnose. I had not seen it in a horse before but there was nothing else it could be. It was in a two year old Arab filly, beautiful and unvaccinated.

I was called to see her in the afternoon and found no external signs of injury, but she did have the early signs of tetanus. She was frightened, stiff, trembling, running a temperature and beginning to dribble from the mouth as she was having difficulty in swallowing. I gave her a massive dose of penicillin, and an anti-tetanus serum – both intravenously – and a sedative. This constitutes the standard treatment for tetanus, which has changed little over the years as nothing else works. I came away from her with no sense other than one of acute foreboding for her welfare.

An early visit next morning confirmed all my worst fears. She was dying with all the horrors of the disease. She was on her side but partially propped up against a bale of straw, which was knocked away every time she had a convulsion. She was unable to swallow due to the 'lock jaw' and she was wide-eyed and terrified. I had no choice but to put her out of her misery just as quickly as I could.

Her owners were distressed and quite unable to understand how the filly could have tetanus without any visible signs of external injury. They had believed like so many others before them that it was all right to leave tetanus vaccination injections until the animal has an injury. Or it may have been the usual syndrome of 'it can't happen to me' – head in sand at work again. Unfortunately it only takes a scratch, perhaps a thorn penetrating somewhere or a cut in the gum, for the tetanus bacillus to enter the tissues and the poison to spread throughout the body. The tetanus germs are all around, in the soil, and are especially thick on the ground where horses graze. They pass hundreds of thousands of the bacillus every time they pass dung so its not surprising a field gets contaminated very quickly.

It makes no sense not to protect the animal as even today, with all the modern treatments and drugs that are available, still only one in a hundred survive clinical symptoms. I have only kept two alive in all my years in horse practice and it makes me pretty mad everytime an animal dies unnecessarily through ignorance or wilful neglect.

I don't want this chapter to turn into a diatribe against horse owners, as pet owners – owners of dogs especially – are just as prone as horse owners to overfeeding their charges. Pony owners are always over-feeding and that can cause severe suffering due to a condition called laminitis, which most of the time is the direct consequence of the animal being overweight. It has been estimated that there are up to eight thousand new cases every year, and as many as twelve thousand at any time are suffering the chronic effects of the disease. Laminitis is where the sensitive part of the foot – the lamina, which is situated between the pedal bone (the last bone in the foot) and the hard outer wall of the hoof becomes inflamed and engorged with blood. It is a very painful disorder that can be very difficult to treat and control. Typically the horse or pony will stand like a rocking horse trying to take as much weight as possible off the front feet, which are usually the most severely affected. If the animal moves at all, it is very slowly and painfully and they tend to shuffle around like an old man wear-ing ill-fitting slippers. I sometimes describe the pain that I think the animal is suffering from as equivalent to that which we feel when we hit ourselves on the nail with a hammer. Bleeding occurs under the nail and it can be excruciatingly painful. How much worse must it be for the animal standing on all four feet when they are all hurt-ing like that?

Laminitis is mostly the result of poor management by an owner, and is most commonly seen in overweight ponies that have been allowed to stuff themselves on grass. This usually happens in the spring when the grass is very rich and at its most lush. It also tends to coincide with the end of the school holidays. If a pony is exercised regularly, then a reasonable diet is required to give it enough energy to keep it going. If, however, it is allowed to eat the same when school has started, and the animal is not getting the same amount of work, then it will get too fat and laminitis is the result.

I can understand a teenager making the mistake of overfeeding and causing distress but I find it much more difficult to take the same fault when experienced owners make the error. People who breed and show ponies always over-feed their animals to get them in what they consider to be 'show condition.' This is just another way of saying overweight or fat and they do it because the judges (breeders as well) will not award rosettes to those animals which are fit but slim! I had a long-standing debate with one owner who would not be convinced that she was wrong about her animal's weight and could not understand why some of her ponies always had a tendency to lameness. It took a very expensive visit to see an equine expert at the Animal Health Trust and a written report before she believed me. Whether it will make any difference in the long-term to the way she feeds is another matter. The risks are high that she could lose a pony if she continues to practice overfeeding as the pedal bone might come through the sole of the foot as the result of chronic laminitis, and when this happens the animal has to be destroyed.

Recent research into the subject of laminitis has changed markedly the way vets treat it. It was thought that standing a patient with sore feet in cold running water did much to alleviate the pain. This is now known to be quite the wrong thing to do. The pony has a much better chance of pain relief, despite the feet being warm to touch, if the feet are immersed in warm water.

The cold water treatment is now as much out of date as bleeding the patient used to be. Bleeding a horse which had laminitis used to be a common practice. This was done by using a fleam – or bleeding knife – which was tapped into the animal's jugular vein, and two to three pints of blood would be removed. This practice reduced the pony's blood pressure for a transitory period and some pain relief would be obtained. It seemed to work and there was some scientific rationale, which was unknown at the time when the technique was commonplace. Drugs are now used to improve the circulation of blood in the foot which, combined with modern pain killers and surgical shoeing, give the best hope for treatment when, through ignorance yet another pony goes down with the condition.

Horses, like people, need to have regular dental checks and you should look after their teeth as if they are your own. Personally I have a conservation order on all my remaining molars, unlike my mother who died just two years ago. She had the same false teeth for over sixty years! Horses and ponies are not so lucky and cannot have false teeth fitted, unlike people and sheep. As far as I know sheep are the only farm-domesticated species that can be fitted with false teeth when their own front incisors fall out. Police and guard dogs can and do have crowns fitted if they lose their canine teeth and they still need to grip and bite with their front teeth.

Horses and rabbits have quite a few things in common including teeth that seem to grow throughout their life. In fact what is happening is that as the teeth wear down, the sockets from which they come are gradually being filled in so that the teeth are being pushed out of the sockets. Because of this, horses and ponies after they are about six years old ought to have their teeth checked at least yearly for sharp edges. If a mouth is sore the animal will not chew properly, which could cause it to bolt its food and have digestive upsets and colic. It is a relatively easy procedure to rasp a horse's molar teeth with an instrument designed for the job. Most vets have evolved their own particular way of doing this. If the patient is fairly quiet, I find that all that is required by way of restraint for the animal is for the handler to hold the horse's tongue out of the side of its mouth. This then allows me to file down the teeth on the opposite side of the mouth without the tongue getting in the way. Occasionally a mouth gag is also required to keep the mouth open as some (ponies are very good at this) are very adept at biting down on the instrument and stopping any further progress. Animals that resent the procedure, and unsurprisingly there are quite a few that do, may require to be twitched. Often to a lay person this seems a barbarous thing to do to an animal and I must admit I used to agree. Twitching involves looping a piece of cord onto the end of the horses nose and then twisting it tight using a short pole-like piece of wood. Doing this nine times out of ten stops any misbehaviour and the job can be done. I used to think this method worked by giving the animal an alternative pain to think about. This doesn't seem to be the case, as the average horse with a twitch applied tends to behave as if it is in a trance. Apparently this is due to the end of the nose being an acupuncture point and the action of the twitch releases endorphins (which are the body's natural painkillers) into the system, which goes a long way to explaining why a correctly applied twitch causes the effect it does. Of course there are times when this method of restraint just does not work and I then resort to giving the patient a sedative injection. Just like some people really. I have at least two veterinary nurses and one vet who have to be sedated before they will go anywhere near a dentist. They have probably been scarred permanently after seeing me at work in a mouth.

One of the last times I was in the dentist chair, I found to my discomfort that one of my back molars required filing down a bit. My dentist, knowing how I rasped horse's teeth, as I have had to deal with his daughter's pony, threatened to treat me in a like manner. I think he meant pulling my tongue out of the side of my mouth, as I couldn't see a twitch in his instrument cupboard. Mind you I often think the suction apparatus is an adequate substitute and he had me more than a little worried for a moment.

You can learn a lot about an animal by looking in its mouth. Telling an animal's age can be simple if you inspect the teeth and note when the milk teeth come out and are replaced by adult fangs. It's not much of a help in cats and dogs as they lose their baby teeth after a few months of age but cattle, sheep and horses can all be accurately aged by checking with dentition charts.

Horses can be aged with reasonable accuracy up to eight years old, but even experienced people can easily make mistakes. A horse's age is very important when it comes to a sale and for example a seven-years-old's teeth can easily be mistaken for a thirteen-year-old's mouth and vice versa. This type of mistake could be disastrous for a buyer as a younger animal is usually worth a lot more than an older one.

Horse dealers, ever since horses could first be bought and sold, have earned a justified reputation for their skill at slightly altering an animal's dental configuration to make them appear younger and therefore more valuable. This is easily done with a file or a rasp. Simply filing off the two small hooks can easily alter a seven – or thirteen-year-old mouth into one that looks a lot younger and it doesn't hurt the animal at all – only the buyer's pocket.

Galvayne's Groove, which gives an indication of a horse's age from ten years old until it is about twenty, can also be rubbed out. At the stroke of a rasp an age can be altered by at least five or six years and this can be very profitable. It is much like 'clocking' a car odometer and knocking off fifty thousand miles. It is just as dishonest and just as illegal. However, new Government legislation means every horse and pony in the land now has to have a passport from birth, which will make life more difficult for the fraudster, but I expect there will be many animals around with dodgy passports and indeterminate ages. Wouldn't it be nice if you could knock five years off your age with a few judicious swipes of a horse file?

While I am still on the subject of teeth, a farmer a few months ago handed me a strange object. It was large – about the size of my hand – and heavy – just over two pounds in weight – with a few crusty deposits all over it. He had found it in a gravel heap, which had been delivered to his yard to patch up a roadway. He was curious about it and asked me what I thought it might be. I could tell from a glance it was a tooth but that was as far as I was able to go. He gave me the object on the understanding I would find out a bit more and report back to him.

On my next half-day off I took the tooth to Cambridge and trawled my way around three separate museums until I found a man with all the answers. I was directed to a large room and on the floor of the room was a mass of different looking objects, some larger and some smaller than my tooth. I showed my trophy to the palaeontologist and asked for an explanation.

He told me at a glance that my tooth was an elephant's premolar.

It was from a young animal and the tooth itself was about seventy thousand years old – give or take a few years. I nearly asked him what it had been eating when it died and I suspect he might have been able to tell me. The gravel and tooth had been extracted from a gravel pit in the Peterborough area and it was apparently a quite well known site for such relics. It seems a lot of elephants had died at that place all those years ago. I had never really believed in elephants' graveyards until now but that chap certainly seemed to know what he was talking about. He had just got back from Siberia where he had been examining similar sites and the specimens on his floor were teeth from elephants and mammoths, which had been excavated from the permafrost.

I got to keep the tooth. The farmer was only interested in the explanation and I will eventually give it to my daughter, who is a dentist. At least I have never been required to extract a tooth that size from an animal's mouth.

Which brings me quite nicely to the subject of Creamy. Creamy was a thirty-five-year-old pony with a problem. Her teeth had been somewhat neglected over the years as she grew older, and old horses are very prone to teeth trouble due to uneven wear if they are not checked on a regular basis.

Creamy was dropping more food out of her mouth as she chewed than she was able to swallow and as a result was getting to look very old and thin. A quick glance at her mouth was not very helpful as the old girl was head shy and would not allow me to examine her properly. After a dose of sedative, I put a mouth gag in place and had a good look. There was a large hook on the sixth molar right at the back of the lower jaw. I had difficulty in seeing it but could feel it quite easily. With the pony very sleepy and the mouth gag in position I could safely put my hand and part of my arm inside her mouth. The hook was long, thick and had a sharp point. It was almost impossible for her to chew anything without excruciating pain.

Hooks like these are impossible to rasp properly and I needed an instrument to cut off the hook. I went back to the surgery knowing I did not have anything suitable. I pored over an instrument catalogue hoping to find the answer to my dilemma and Creamy's hook. There was none, but I remembered my collection of old veterinary instruments. I had long looked at a long, thin rod with a notch at one end. I had no idea for what purpose it was originally made but as I took it from the display cabinet it occurred to me that I might just be able to use it to knock off the offending protuberance. The procedure would not be without some risk. I was concerned that I might crack the molar but I could not let Creamy carry on the way she was – slowly starving to death. I was also concerned that any dislodged particle of tooth might fall into the back of the throat and be inhaled into the windpipe.

I went back to see Creamy two days later, armed with my 'new' piece of equipment. I followed the usual procedure and sedated the old girl again with a dose of Domesedan. As usual it didn't take very much – although lively and difficult to catch, she seemed thinner than ever.

I placed the mouth gag into position and once more felt for the offending tooth. It was even longer and thicker than I remembered and I thought once again of the consequences if things went wrong. I couldn't bring myself to attempt to knock it off! All too clearly I could foresee the worst danger and the likely consequences of failure. If the instrument slipped the metal rod would penetrate the soft tissue at the back of the throat and cause a fatal haemorrhage.

I have this maxim at moments of crisis: if you are not sure you are going to do some good, then don't do it!

So I didn't do as I had planned but I had to do something. I could have referred her to an equine clinic for surgery but the owner wasn't prepared to do this due to the cost involved and the likelihood of her not surviving a general anaesthetic. To do nothing was not an option. Euthanasia was the only other alternative.

I had with me a pair of long-handled dental forceps, which I thought I might have to use if all else failed. I reached as far into the mouth as possible with the instrument and managed to get a grip on the molar but only just. I had no great hopes that I would be able to extract the tooth as equine molars have very long roots, but I had to try. I applied the maximum pressure I could and pulled and twisted. With a crunching noise that I seem to be able to recall every time I submit myself to dental treatment, it came out. I deposited the offending article into the owner's outstretched hand. I don't know who was more pleased, him or me, but Creamy couldn't have cared less as she was still asleep on her feet.

When she did waken there was no doubt she could, despite just having a tooth extracted, chew and swallow with greater comfort. I hoped she would soon gain weight and enjoy a more comfortable retirement in her orchard paddock. But it was not to be. After a few more weeks it became apparent that she was not going to put on any more weight and we decided to end her life before she became too debilitated.

It was a sad end for her and very sad for her owners. She had been a very 'hot' gymkhana pony in her youth, winning trophies far and wide. She had been much loved and pampered when she was active but in retirement, although fed and talked to every day, in other respects she had been somewhat neglected. She should have had her teeth checked regularly. If this had been done then Creamy might have lived much longer and may even have beaten the practice record for equine longevity, set by a pony that died quietly in her sleep at the grand old age of forty-five.

Treating horses of any age and size is always a bit dangerous – to the animal and to the vet and nurse involved. This is especially true when a horse or pony has to have an operation, which requires a general anaesthetic. Specialist equine hospitals and units have operating theatres that are the last word in sophistication. They mostly all have the most up to date equipment to try and ensure the animal's safety but still there is a higher than normal risk of something going wrong either before the surgical procedure, when the animal is being anaesthetised, or afterwards during recovery. This is due to the size of the beasts and the comparative fragility of the long leg bones. Getting a horse safely into a horizontal position and asleep and then reversing the process, despite heavily padded recovery rooms is always a worry for both owners and the surgical team. Despite many improvements in modern anaesthetic drugs a horse during recovery is still liable to crash around more than a bit when it is trying to get on its feet again.

Although I have carried out a great many surgical procedures on horses under general anaesthetic I have never aspired to having an equine operating theatre. This is because the costs involved in building and staffing such a unit can only be justified by specialist vets who do nothing else but horse work, and much of that comes from referral of difficult cases from general practitioners like myself.

I have always anaesthetised horses in grass filled paddocks. This is typically done when castrating young colts or suturing wounds that cannot be attended to under sedation and local anaesthetic. It is cheaper for the client to have operations done in this way if it is at all possible but of course it can only be done if the weather and the ground is suitable. I don't like operating in the rain and it's not much good for the patient either.

I have been most fortunate over the years that I have never suffered a fatality operating in this way but it is always a worry that something might go wrong.

The nearest I ever got to a disaster was when I operated on a very large Percheron stallion called Sam. It was fair to say that Sam was in the twilight of his years – getting on for twenty years old. He was an All England champion stallion, having been judged as the best in his breed more than a few times at the Royal Show, the Royal Norfolk Show and the East of England Show. He was very large, being easily over one tonne in weight, and he developed a large, cancerous testicle. It did not seem to cause him any pain but as the lesion got larger it became ulcerated and started to attract flies. Something had to be done and I agreed with his owner, Dick, that we should give Sam one last chance to beat the cancer, and I would operate to remove the cancerous growth.

Sam received the standard dose of anaesthetic for his weight and lay down with a bit of a crash on the soft ground of his paddock. The operation went without a hitch and the testicle was removed. It almost needed a wheelbarrow to take it away. Sam's other testicle was totally normal and he lay on the ground completely oblivious to the drama in which he was the central, unwitting player. After all the sutures were in place it was time for Sam to waken from his slumbers. I have for years used a drug called Immobilon to anaesthetise horses. Although it does have its disadvantages being a derivative of morphine, the one great property it has is that the effect of the drug can be reversed within minutes by giving an intravenous injection of an antagonist called Revivon. Sam was given his dose of Revivon and woke up within five minutes but despite all sorts of encouragement and cajoling would not stand up. We waited a few more minutes and gave him something to eat, which he accepted very happily, but he was quite content to stay where he was – sitting up but not about to stand for anybody.

I gave him some more antidote, to no effect, and eventually left him sitting comfortably and his owner worrying while I carried on with my morning round. A telephone message came in from Dick a few hours later to say that Sam still refused to stand. This by now was getting serious as a large animal like Sam would very soon have muscle and skin damage due to pressure sores. If he didn't get up soon he would never rise again and his operation would have been all for nothing.

A colleague was dispatched on my behalf and gave the horse a large dose of a stimulant drug normally only used in dogs and cats. It worked, or maybe Sam had by now had enough fuss and rest, and he almost immediately stood up. He was a bit shaky but he was fine and when I saw him next day he was back to being his old self. A few months on he was positively gleaming with health and actually sired another foal. He died two years later when he was found cast

in his stable and had to be put down. Despite his sad end the operation had been worthwhile and worth the risk, and I think Sam
would have agreed if the choice had been his to make.

CHAPTER 11

In Memory of Saffron

SHE KNEW I HAD come to kill her. As soon as I opened the door and came into the room where she lay on an unmade, unruly bed, I knew she knew. I could tell by the look in her dull, pain-filled eyes that she knew. She was frightened. She had never been scared of me before.

We had lived together for about seven years. I took her in after her first home became unsuitable as her companion was out all day at work and Saffron did not like her own company very much. We came to know each other very well. I loved her and I think the feelings were reciprocated, although she never said.

I had seen her frightened before. She had an irrational fear of thunder – storms and lightning – and was terrified by heavy rain. I came home late one night while thunder was rumbling around the Fens and I could not find her. Eventually she was discovered, completely hidden under some bedclothes and whimpering quietly. Her eyes looked then as they did now. They had lost their twinkle and looked more like lazy coals – tired and hoping for oblivion.

That night took all my patience and reassurance to calm her.

I stayed with her on her bed – we never slept together normally – until the next morning when all the threat from the skies had gone and she had fallen into a sound sleep. Next day she was her old self again, bright and happy, and nothing was said about the previous evening. She had probably forgotten – that was how she coped with life; that was Saffron.

Now – again – she was lying on her bed and she was frightened. We had been friends for most of her adult life and it was the first time she wasn't glad to see me. I scared her. She knew her friend had come to kill her.

She lay back on the cushion that served as a pillow, not able to tell me what she really thought. Would she be grateful for a release from the pain, which was with her every sleepless moment of her present existence? And then there was the smell. It had come gradually since the diagnosis of carcinoma had confirmed our worst fears, and was now becoming overwhelming. It was a rank, foetid smell that told of her shaming – to her – incontinence. Even now, with all the care she was having, her bedding was dampened in places by urine.

I knelt beside her and spoke in a soft, soothing way – the usual nonsense.

'It's all right, don't worry, you'll be OK,' I said, while I stroked her hair, patted her cheek and tried to reassure her in any way I could that all was well.

I was still her friend – even though I had come to end her life here and now in this small, cheerless, depressing, little room with its fading wallpaper and peeling magnolia paint, that once was as bright and fresh as her eyes when she was young.

She was a sixties child, this Saffron, her manner typical of the time. Blond, long-haired, careless of her appearance but confident that she was liked and loved by all who knew her. She never seemed to bother about material things. When she came to stay, she had brought very little with her. She ate only now and again when she felt inclined but certainly with no regular pattern. It was the way she managed to keep her sylph-like figure when all her contemporaries had long since succumbed to a comfortable middle aged spread.

Years ago, when she had first come to live with me, we went on holiday took a long walk over some broad, bare, Border hills. We were away all day, sharing our drink and food and revelling in the space and peace of the countryside. Sometimes when I was flagging she would pull me up a slope and then – laughing – chase me down the other side, her long hair streaming behind her in the wind.

When we got back to the cottage that night, starving hungry, we ate and fell asleep together by the fireside.

When she was much younger she had two puppies, a male and female, and she was so proud of them. She fed them well but let them go without fussing when it was their time to find their own place in the world. She never had any more offspring despite her sixties tendency to be rather free with her favours.

She groaned a little and touched my arm with her paw and brought me back to the chilling reality of the moment. I wondered if I had the strength to do what I had come to do.

But I had to for her sake. I could not bear to see her in this agony and with her surroundings getting increasingly squalid. It was the last caring thing I could do for her – to put an end to her suffering. But now I frightened her, as she knew all too well what I had to do.

We had all agreed – all those who cared for her – that we could not let her suffer any longer. We were sure that if she had been able to give an opinion she would have agreed. And it had fallen to me. I was after all qualified to insert a needle into a vein.

I had been avoiding looking directly at her and into her eyes. I knew they were brown; a deep, dark, mahogany brown and they were watching my every move. I did not look at her as I thought she might see in my eyes my own pain and uncertainty as I prepared to end her life, and I did not wish to add to her distress.

I was wrong. When I eventually did look straight at her, as I caressed her face and spoke quietly she suddenly seemed to calm and be less afraid. We were alone together – no one else could bear to witness what I was about to do. I could delay no longer.

I opened my bag and took out a ten millilitre plastic syringe, and coupled it to a green shafted twenty-one by five-eighths needle. I grasped the blue covered bottle of pentobarbitone in my left hand and inserted the needle through the rubber top with my right. The plunger on the syringe was withdrawn and the instrument filled with the deadly liquid.

Saffron seemed to be watching with more detachment than fear now that the moment had arrived. A bottle of surgical spirit was inverted over a plug of cotton wool until it was saturated. A tourniquet was the last item required, and I placed it above her elbow and then tightened. The cephalic vein swam into view and it had to be done.

I uttered a short prayed under my breath.

'Please don't let me miss the vein,' I said.

I had to keep my hand steady, my eyes tear free, and concentrate on what I was doing for her sake. My aim was perfect. Red, angry blood pulsed back into the barrel of the syringe and mixed with the blue drug. I released the tourniquet and pressed the plunger. The blood and poison disappeared into her body.

I removed the needle and could do nothing more but hold her head and wait the five long seconds for the pentobarbitone to conduct its fatal business.

She knew – at the end – it was best – I think.

She, with her last movement, tried to lick my hand. Her tail flickered so very slightly and then her eyes darkened as death dilated her pupils. Her legs stretched then relaxed and she was gone.

Saffron, the Golden Retriever bitch died as peacefully as I hope one day to die – asleep and in her bed. But no one will press the plunger for me. I'm only human and people do not have the same privileges that are accorded to much loved pets.

This is where I am now when it comes to euthanasia but at the beginning of my veterinary career I had a robust no-nonsense attitude to killing an animal. It came from having a farming background. Life and death were very much a part of the environment and treated in a natural, matter of fact manner. I was first made aware that not everyone shared my lack of sensibilities when I was 'seeing practice' as a student. I was with the vet, doing his morning rounds, and he had been called to a house to attend a sick dog. This had been duly and satisfactorily sorted out when, en route to the car through the garden, the dog's owner noticed an injured bird on the pathway. He picked it up and asked me to look after it. A moment's glance told me it would never fly again and I quickly and somewhat expertly broke its neck and put it out of its misery. I was then very much taken to task by the owner, who had expected me to carry it off and 'take care of it properly.' The vet later, in private, told me I had done the right thing but at the wrong time as I had not considered the client's feelings.

This need to be more aware of a client's finer feelings was reinforced some weeks later when I had to accompany another veterinary surgeon to an old lady's house in Peebles, to see a sick budgie. As bad luck would have it, the bird had an inoperable tumour and had to be put down. The lady was heart broken, as this little animal was the only company she had since her husband died. She loved it and she was going to miss it dreadfully. It was a very bare room in a small house, lacking most of the usual amenities, and it was made to feel all the more bleak by her tears. We took every care to comfort her before we removed the budgie and humanely ended its life with chloroform. The vet wrote to her afterwards and explained again why her pet had to die and was rewarded with a charming letter in return thanking him for his care. That one case told me more about how to handle grief and how to be more aware of people's feelings when a pet has to be put down than any number of lectures.

For many people, their dog, cat or even rat is to them a faithful companion, a member of the family and often a child substitute. When a pet has to die – and very few die naturally in their sleep – an owner will usually feel a mixture of emotions from grief to anger, and often guilt. The frequently asked question is:

'Would it have made any difference if I had called you in sooner?'

Sometimes the honest answer would be 'yes,' but I don't often say so, as that would not serve any useful purpose unless another animal is at risk.

It is often very difficult to gauge how different people will react to their pets dying. Some are seemingly indifferent and outwardly callous, but a joking demeanour can often be a mask that hides deep distress. Not long after the Falklands campaign a para-trooper came to me with his old dog. It was at least eighteen years old, its teeth were rotten, it was crippled with arthritis and could hardly walk despite being very thin. It had also terminal kidney failure and it was going to be kinder by far to put it to sleep rather than subject it to hospitalisation and treatment, which would at most extend its life by only a few days.

Given this choice the soldier made the sensible decision to put an end to his old friend's life and relieve its suffering. The decision was made in a brusque, off hand manner but when he came to hold the dog for the lethal injection he broke down completely and wept. He said later he had been in the thick of the conflict at Goose Green and had seen both friends and enemies killed but that had not touched him so hard as holding his old dog as it died.

For me personally, I find it much more difficult, as a man, to cope with another man in tears. The male is brought up to hold the ethos that it is unmanly to cry, and when he does he is often embarrassed as well as being distressed for his pet. Women cry more readily, without shame and I know that this release of emotion is healthy and essential to help them mourn properly for their pet. Mourning a much loved pet is as normal and necessary as grieving for a human and it's a shame that so many men are often ashamed to admit their feelings.

I suppose that most people feel that the vet's job is done when the syringe is empty and the animal is dead but I find that this is often very far from being the case. Apart from writing a letter, which is mostly to reassure the owner that their decision was the correct one for their pet, and that to have delayed any longer would only have increased the animal's suffering, we as a practice are often involved with the funeral arrangements. Many owners wish to have their animals cremated and have their ashes returned, and this we can and do organise. There was a time when it was not uncommon for an owner to have their dear departed stuffed, and I did have the telephone number of a local taxidermist to hand. I always thought taxidermy was a bit strange and was amazed when my mother wanted her dead cat immortalised in this way, but I managed to persuade her to do otherwise and give it a woodland burial instead.

Other grieving owners ask undertakers to make proper coffins for their pets and attend to arrangements for them. Indeed there are now companies whose entire business it is to organise coffins and burials for any pet, large or small, from a cat to a horse. A client some years ago made his own pets' coffins in solid oak. They were very robust structures, and they needed to be as when he moved house, as he did twice while I knew him, the coffins were exhumed, put in the removal van and reburied in the new garden!

My most enduring memory of a dog's funeral was for a gun dog owned by a close friend. Old Bob had served my friend well over many years and when he was put down he was buried with full shooting honours under the chestnut tree in the back garden. I was invited to attend and was asked to fire a shot over his grave as a parting salute. This I did with all due solemnity, and was nudged by my friend to do the job properly by firing the second barrel from the shot-gun. We then retired to the front parlour to drink a toast to the memory of Old Bob and retell many of his exploits.

What I have talked about so far in this context has been the euthanasia of mostly dogs and birds, but I have to admit that for me the hardest job of all is to put down a horse or pony. It really – rationally – should not make any difference. Horses or ponies are euthanased by me for the same reasons as for other pet animals. They may be in pain, which cannot be relieved due to a shattered limb or twisted bowel, or just very old and terminally ill.

It may be the method that is used that upsets me the most, which is still mostly a gunshot, but whatever the reason and however correct the decision, when it comes to putting the gun between the brown and trusting eyes and pulling the trigger I always feel physically sick. It's not rational of me, I know.

An injection can be used, which will do the job but much more slowly, and a bullet causes instant oblivion, but I hate having to perform this often very necessary service.

As you might expect, however, even with death as a subject, there are some lighter moments. All veterinary practices have their share of eccentric clients but very few compare with the one gentleman who shuffled through our doorway some years ago, dragging an old dog behind him. He was a man of about sixty years of age with a somewhat dishevelled appearance, a belligerent expression and a loud voice, probably because he was a bit deaf. He came up to the reception desk and I could tell from his manner that he was going to give the on-duty nurse a difficult time. Anticipating this I intercepted him and asked if I could help.

'Yes,' was the reply, 'I want my dog done in.'

There was a time when we might have agreed to his request without further question but not anymore. We always like to find out the reason for the request first, before anything is done. Automatic euthanasias are not part and parcel of veterinary life anymore. I took him to a nearby consulting room to question him further, as it is often possible to re-home an unwanted pet. Safely within the privacy of the room I asked, 'What's the matter with the dog?'

The old dog looked up at me and wagged his tail, which was a distinct improvement on the owner's expression.

'Well master,' he said, prodding me in the chest with his fore-finger, 'It's not the dog, it's the vacuum cleaner that's the problem. My old Hoover has broken down. I've got a new one but it's no good, the dog has got to go.' I had some difficulty in making the connection between dog and cleaner but he soon explained in his inimitable manner.

It seemed that until it had broken down, his old cleaner would pick up the dog dirt in the house – these were not quite the words he used but I expect you will get the general idea. He had tried to get the old machine repaired but to no avail as the repair-man, strangely enough, would not touch it. He had bought a new cleaner and tried that but it was no good, as it wouldn't pick up like the old one. He even complained to the shop where he had bought the new machine but there was nothing else they could do and, 'NO,' they would not refund his money!

Faced with an obviously incontinent old dog whose re-homing prospects were nil, it was obvious the old thing would have to go. I agreed to his request and asked him to put the dog on the table.

'No, no mate,' came the reply, 'I can't do that yet, I've only just bought a load of dog food and it's got to eat that first!'

With that he turned around and, dragging the old mongrel behind him, which strangely enough was still wagging its tail, went off down the drive, audibly muttering and complaining about British work-manship and new cleaners.

I wasn't too surprised that he and his dog failed to keep the appointment for the following week and I never saw him or his faithful mutt again.

CHAPTER 12

On Official Duty

MOST VETERINARY SURGEONS IN private practice, especially if they are in farm practice, are called on from time to time to act in some official capacity in one way or another. Most vets in agricultural, or mixed practices as they are known, are like me sort of part time veterinary officers for the Ministry of Agriculture now known as DEFRA (Department of Environment, Food and Rural Affairs).

As such the private vet has a huge role in the attempt to control and eradicate many of the animal diseases which can also affect people. These diseases, such as Tuberculosis, Brucellosis and Anthrax, are notifiable diseases, which means that if a stockman or farmer, as well as a vet, suspects the presence of any of these diseases then they must by law inform the police or the local veterinary officer employed by DEFRA. Deliberately withholding information can result in prosecution. In many cases ignorance for once can be a legitimate excuse, but not if you are a vet. Some years ago a colleague asked me to perform a post-mortem on a sow that had died in his area. It had been a dreadfully busy day and I did not reach the knacker yard until almost eight o'clock in the evening. By this time the knacker men had been at work dismembering the animal, as they had not been told that we were coming to look at the beast. All that was left that could be looked at was a very enlarged spleen. I took a swab from the organ and plated the material onto a blood agar plate, then put it into the incubator at the surgery and almost immediately forgot about it. Prompted by my partner next afternoon, I looked at the plate and discovered to my horror the typical 'medusa head' growth that could only be Anthrax. A very rapid call to the then Ministry of Agriculture brought out the Divisional Veterinary Officer who confirmed my diagnosis. He promptly shut down the knacker yard and put all the workers there on antibiotics for a week. All was well in the end, with no harm done but I could very easily not have taken the swab and Anthrax spores could have been spread over a wide area. In the end I was commended for being very alert and spotting the risk but an outbreak of the disease was very close to being missed altogether.

If there is an outbreak of a notifiable disease such as Foot and Mouth disease, Swine Fever, Fowl Pest or – to be topical – Avian Flu, ministry vets will take charge of the full time operation, to attempt to bring any such outbreak under control. They have widespread powers to isolate and quarantine premises and animals and slaughter diseased, infected or dangerous-contact animals. However, there are many occasions when a disease is so widespread that there are just not enough ministry vets to be able to cope, and vets in private practice are asked to assist the official vets. This has happened frequently in the past and most people will remember the dreadful outbreak of Foot and Mouth disease in the United Kingdom of two years ago. Nearly all the large animal vets in the country were mobilised at one time or another to help contain the outbreak. The outbreak came close to destroying the farming industry in this country and many farmers became totally disheartened and, disillusioned, sold their farms and left the land altogether.

Every month most agricultural practices are sent lists of farms where the animals have to be tested for Brucellosis and or Tuberculosis. Tuberculosis used to be a terrible scourge of animals and people in this country. Years ago the most likely cause of the infection in people was directly from cows, by drinking infected milk or as result of man to man infection by inhalation – aided by terrible hygiene, ignorance and poor ventilation in overcrowded houses. Now the disease is mostly under control due to the rigorous testing of cattle, although it is still a problem in the southwest of the country where many herds are continually being re-infected by badgers. Milk for a long time has not been a source of infection as long as it has been pasteurised, as this process kills the tuberculin bacillus.

Routine testing of cattle has for the most part contained Tuberculosis, and intra-dermal testing is still the only reliable test for the disease in the living animal. The skin of the neck is clipped in two places, above and below each other and the skin thickness is measured with callipers. A very small amount (0.1 ml) of killed avian and killed bovine tuberculin is injected into the skin at the prepared sites. The tuberculin inoculation has to be killed otherwise it would infect the animal but it is enough to cause a reaction in an infected beast. The cattle are re-examined after three days when the skin thickness is measured again. If the skin reaction on the bovine site is greater than the avian then the beast may well have tuberculosis and will have to be slaughtered. The farmer will be compensated for any animals lost in this way.

It's a boring, repetitive, but vital job for the vet but if the farmer is well organised even a large number of cattle can be examined in a day. Providing the vet is not stressed by having other visits to attend and the weather is pleasant then tuberculin testing can be viewed as a bit of a holiday away from the stresses and strains of the practice. James Herriott – in real life Alf Wight – seemed to see it this way as he took his new bride tuberculin testing in the Dales instead of going away on honeymoon. Now that is taking things a bit too far, even if the practice was getting behind with clearing up the list of farms to be checked.

Tuberculosis in badgers remains a headache as it is considered that they are the main source of re-infection for cattle. It must be very disheartening for farmers to have their animals declared tuberculin free only for them to have more reactors after a few months. Trying to eradicate the badgers from a farm is not the answer, as this seems to disseminate infection around the district. It is not always possible to kill every badger in the set and even if this is possible other badgers will quickly recolonise an empty burrow. I hope in the future it will be possible to give all badgers that are in a high risk area an oral vaccine. This may be the best way forward in finally eradicating tuberculosis as the scourge of the cattle industry.

Brucellosis is another notifiable disease, which has largely been eradicated in the United Kingdom over the last thirty years. This has been done by identifying animals with the infection by blood test, and slaughtering all those identified as having the disease. The disease causes abortion in cattle and undulant fever in man. It is a bacterial infection, which is especially nasty in humans as it causes an intermittent high fever and a general feeling of being unwell that can go on for months. Quite a few of my colleagues have suffered from its effects over the years as when the infection was present in most of the national herd the profession was most at risk by treating cows that had aborted and retained their placentas. When I joined the practice as a young vet, unknown to myself and everyone else one of the partners was suffering from the disease. He had felt unwell for some time and it was thought he had a heart condition. He decided to give up the rigours of general practice and retire to the more sedate life of a government vet working in a laboratory. He sold his share of the practice to me only to discover a few months later that he had Brucellosis. Another vet at the laboratory where he was working suggested he have a blood test and it came out positive. He had a two to three month period of intensive antibiotic treatment and was cured. He could have stayed in the practice but his loss was my gain and for both of us there was no going back. My professional life in the Fens of Cambridgeshire and Norfolk was the result of a Brucellosis infection, but fortunately not in me.

These two diseases are only an example of the many infectious diseases that we have to deal with as part of our routine work and also as 'official' vets. We are fortunate, as I write, that we do not have Foot and Mouth disease, Swine Fever or Rabies present in

Britain at the moment, unless you count the possibility of Rabies in some bats. This doesn't mean the diseases won't come back and we as a profession must keep up our guard at all times against the possibility of fresh outbreaks.

The idea of Rabies coming back to this country and becoming endemic in the wildlife fills me with horror. A walk or picnic in the countryside would never be the same again if we had to continuously be on our guard against rabid animals. Contrary to what most people will believe a fox – or it could just as easily be a squirrel or a badger – if infected with Rabies would be unlikely to rush out of the undergrowth, foaming at the mouth. It is much more likely to have the dumb form of the disease where it loses all fear of people and could easily be fondled by a child. Quarantine restrictions are still in place for all dogs, cats, rats, mice, guinea pigs, and the rest where they originate in the near East, Far East and Africa, as the disease is so out of control in these areas. This means that when they enter the United Kingdom, dogs and cats have to be vaccinated against Rabies and they all have to do six months quarantine. Animals originating from the Common Market countries, the United States and island countries such as Australia, New Zealand and Japan can avoid quarantine restrictions providing they have a pet passport. This properly identifies each individual animal and certifies that it has been correctly vaccinated against the disease, with blood test results to prove it. The pet passport scheme also means that pets can accompany owners to the continent on holiday or to pet shows, or for breeding purposes, and return to Britain without quarantine restrictions applying.

The pet passport system is working well at the present time but I hope we don't become too complacent. It would only take one infected animal for the whole system to fall apart and human lives might be at risk.

I am in charge of a quarantine kennel and although most owners hate to see their animals closely confined, both cats and dogs usually settle down well after the first few days of feeling strange. One of my colleagues or I have to attend the kennels every day apart from Sundays and bank holidays, and we are always on call every day, twenty-four hours a day, in case of emergency. Very occasionally a cat will be distressed and aggressive for a few days and then settle down. One youngster came by sea on a yacht from Hong Kong. It was a kitten when it left the Far East but fully grown by the time it arrived in the UK. It had only ever known a heaving deck and its two owners, and it was more than a little disoriented when it arrived. It was extremely aggressive for the first few days – in fact it would attack anyone brave enough to go near it. I'm sure the ground was still spinning around but it soon settled down to being one of the sweetest-natured cats in the whole cattery.

It is not unusual for both cats and dogs to give birth while in quarantine. This usually goes well and although the mother has to complete the six months, the offspring are allowed out after they are old enough to be weaned.

If an animal dies while still in quarantine, its brain has to be examined for any evidence of the virus that caused the disease. There is a good vaccination against Rabies, which is very effective but once clinical symptoms appear there is no cure for the sufferer, whether animal or man, and they die in a horrible way.

Animals, both domestic and farm, are exported all over the world from Britain as a very regular occurrence and it all helps to keep the British economy thriving. These animals have to be healthy and may have to have blood and faecal tests to comply with the health requirements of the importing country. This is also the case with semen, which is exported from bulls and boars to all over the world, and I spend a lot of time fighting my way through official forms to facilitate the easy passage of animals and semen to many different parts of the globe.

Local veterinary inspectors are also involved in abattoirs on meat inspection duties, which are vital for the health of the nation. Before the animal is slaughtered for human consumption it has to be seen alive for a health check, and all meat inspection carried out is under veterinary authority. In the same way all livestock markets have to be visited by experienced vets to ensure that only healthy animals are being sold and that they are fit to travel onward to the next farm.

To enable us private vets to carry out these duties we have to be licensed by DEFRA and have a warrant card to produce when necessary. This can allow us to enter premises and take such samples as are thought to be required for the purpose of examining and treating animals which may have a notifiable disease. More strangely we are also given the authority to dig up (notwithstanding the Animal Health Act of 1984, which this prohibits) any carcass or part of a carcass, which is thought to be expedient to determine the cause of the death.

Other 'official' occasions for the local vet include attendance, usually in an honorary capacity (which means you might be lucky and get a free lunch) at the local agricultural show. This, unless the vet has a particular expertise with a particular breed of animal and is judging some of the classes, generally means being on call for any medical emergencies. At one particular show ground I had to measure ponies and horses for their different classes every year. This was a farcical procedure as to measure a horse properly it has to be relaxed and unworried to get a fair indication of its height. I found this nigh on impossible as the flat measuring pad was in full view of all passing traffic, including animals on their way to the ring. It was also a cause of much friction with owners who were never convinced, despite the show regulations, that the rule was meant to be enforced and that their animals were not exempt.

As a young vet I approached these local shows with some misgiving, not to say trepidation, believing in all the horror stories of the many pitfalls that await the inexperienced. My senior partner, Alec Noble, helped to calm my fears and put me right in so many ways, but the vet who helped me most in this respect lived and worked in the neighbouring town of Whittlesey and in fact was the opposition practice.

Sam Poles was one of the finest clinicians and veterinary surgeons of the old school that I had the privilege of knowing, and he died about fifteen years ago much lamented by all his old friends and clients. He was not a man to suffer fools gladly but he often went out of his way to give advice to and help the genuinely troubled owner or colleague who sought his assistance and advice. Nor was he over ready to send in a bill, which endeared him to many more people. He was also inclined to take payment for his bill from a farmer in the form of a load of hay or straw.

There is a wealth of stories and legends told about him, probably mostly apocryphal, but some must be true and I can vouch for the following, as a bank manager who observed it first hand told me.

Many years ago, the most popular entertainment at an agricultural show, apart from the displays of livestock and the beer tent, were the trotting races. These races were generally held after the grand parade of all the prize-winners, from the middle part of the afternoon until the show closed. This activity has now been largely superseded by show jumping, which I consider a much inferior spectator sport.

The organising committee of the show would hire a promoter, who would turn up on the appointed afternoon with the necessary horses, jockeys and all the other accoutrements, and races would be run. It was always a splendid spectacle with much noise and colour, dust or mud flying everywhere depending on the whim of the weather. It always evoked memories of 'Ben Hur' or the Calgary Stampede on impressionable onlookers like myself.

I do think the main reason the event was so popular was that it gave the members of the public the opportunity to bet on the outcome of each race. Why this should have been I could never quite fathom, as even at a tender age I was quite cynical about such matters and I always understood that the bookmakers worked hand in glove with the promoter. There was very little profit to be had even by those 'in the know.'

Sam Poles had for many years been the honorary veterinary

surgeon to the show. He would be present all day on the day and attend to any animals that required veterinary attention. If he was lucky he would get a decent lunch and a drink for his trouble.

One particular show day, during the first race, one of the trotting horses sustained a cut on its leg and a request was made for veterinary assistance. Sam duly obliged and examined the animal to find it required a few stitches in the wound. This was done and the grateful promoter asked Sam how much he owed for his professional services.

'Oh no,' was the reply, 'I am proud to be the honorary veterinary surgeon to the show and as such I am only too pleased and happy to do this for your horse free of charge. However,' he continued (sotto voce) 'if you would like to give your opinion as to who might win the next race?'

He left the aside in the air and was duly and discreetly rewarded with a name.

The next race was soon over and after Sam had collected his winnings from the puzzled bookmaker he had a further thought, that perhaps he ought to administer an anti-tetanus injection to the injured horse. He checked the animal again and the very pleased and gratified owner asked him again how much he owed Sam for the injection. The reply, not surprisingly, was the same as the previous time.

'I wouldn't hear of charging you for this. As you know I am the honorary veterinary surgeon to the show and I am only too pleased to be of assistance.'

He let the aside go by this time but again received the tip for the outcome of the next race. The afternoon proceeded in a like manner as after every race further visits were made to ensure the welfare of his patient. Such goings on would not be tolerated these days but it all happened a long time ago and no one was a bit upset or put out, except for the bookmakers who for once lost a packet and never knew the reason.

Vets have to attend all horse race meetings, and also races at greyhound stadiums, where these are under the control of the National Greyhound Racing Association. As official vet at a racing track, one's behaviour has to be above suspicion and reproach. As a matter of course all staff are not allowed to bet on the outcome of any race, in case they are tempted to take some action that might alter it – and that includes the vet!

My practice used to attend at the local greyhound track on a regular basis – three nights a week – and our duties as vets started about six thirty in the evening. We had to be there that early as all the runners for the evening had to be checked before they were kennelled. There were usually about sixty dogs altogether and each one had to be examined to make sure it was not lame and was in a fit state to run. This was done between six thirty and seven fifteen as the first race started at seven thirty pm. As well as the veterinary inspection, the dogs had to be weighed and positively identified before being locked away securely in individual kennels until it was their turn to race.

The reason behind all this checking was to try and ensure that all races were fair and above board and that no dog was subjected to any activity which would make it run slower or faster than its natural ability and fitness. Or in other words, to prevent 'nobbling.'

Over the years the general public's perception of greyhound racing has been that much of it is blemished by owners or trainers, or sometimes outsiders with betting interests, doping the dogs to alter their racing performances. While this is by no means as common as many think, tampering or interfering with racing dogs does go on.

A common method of doing this is to reduce a dog's performance by some means over a few races and then, when the chosen race comes along, to allow the dog to run to its true potential and win the race. This can be accomplished quite easily, without using drugs, by altering some part of its training or feeding schedule. The racing odds on a dog having had a few poor performances are good and therefore when it wins unexpectedly a lot of money can be made from the bookmaker.

Naturally when a dog runs much better or worse than the formbook suggests, questions are asked and very often samples are taken for drug testing. Anyone found guilty of a misdemeanour in this way is banned from the track, and the National Greyhound Racing Association bans any trainers found guilty of 'nobbling' in any way from training.

I must emphasise again, in case I give a thoroughly wrong impression, that the vast majority of owners and trainers are very honest and would not be involved in any activities or illegal schemes, which might harm their dogs.

However, despite the risks to man and dog, interfering with a racing dog still goes on occasionally, particularly on unlicensed (known as flapping) tracks. The last method I heard of for stopping, that is to say 'slowing', a dog that I came across while I was still an official at the track was to spray a flea-spray into the dog's kennel after it had been inspected. In the narrow confines of the kennel this adversely affected the atmosphere and the dog's performance was slightly impaired. This method is virtually foolproof unless you catch the perpetrator in the act, as most greyhounds are treated regularly for fleas anyway. Eternal vigilance is the only way to try and combat the cheat but every now and again the unexpected can and does happen – and one night it did.

It was a big race night with lots of prize money at stake and there was a large, expectant crowd. The stadium was buzzing with barely suppressed excitement and activity around the book-makers' pitches as it got nearer to the main event of the evening: the area final. There was a lot of money and prestige at stake.

After each preceding race is run the security steward has to walk around the perimeter of the track to ensure all is well and safe before the next race. He especially makes sure that the perimeter fence is secure, and on this particular racetrack it was a corrugated iron fence. His final task before the next race is to replace the mechanical hare (known to all in the greyhound fraternity as the 'bunny') on the running rail and get it into position and ready for the off.

For the big race the dogs were paraded in front of the grand-stand as usual, to give the punters one last look at the runners before they were loaded into the starting traps. The starter checked to see that all was well and set the hare off running. The dogs in the traps yelped in anticipation, the crowd roared, and when the hare passed the traps the dogs were released and the race was on. The runners had two circuits of the track to run but half way around the second lap the race came to a shuddering halt as the hare fell off its rail!

The story behind the technical problem was revealed to me somewhat later. Apparently the wrong dog had been winning from a betting syndicate's point of view and an agreed signal had gone out to an accomplice who had been hiding behind the fence for just such an emergency. At the agreed signal he had thrust a stick through a convenient hole in the corrugated fence and knocked the bunny off the rail as it rushed passed.

The race had to be declared null and void, to be run another evening and all bets had to be returned. The guilty parties to the plot were suspected but never proved and that evening passed into folklore as the night the hare was 'nobbled' and not the dog.

For a private veterinary surgeon being an 'official' vet from time to time is thought to be a bit dull and the less interesting side of practice, but in my experience it has its moments as well.

CHAPTER 13

The Bitten Bites back

FROM THE TIME WHEN Stone Age man changed from being a hunter of animals to herding them instead, he tried to make them easier to handle and more amenable to domestication. Those nomadic herders must have realised very early on that a castrated animal is much easier to tame than one with all its assets and hormones intact. And how right they were! Now in modern enlightened Britain, castration is seen to be an unnecessary mutilation in some species but still necessary in others. As a young vet I could spend many hours of my day castrating young pigs and calves. Not any more! Although farmers are trained to carry out these procedures themselves, as far as pigs and cattle are concerned it is recognised that these animals grow quicker and are ready for market and slaughter at a much younger age than before if they are left intact.

Although it is impossible to say for sure, it is quite likely that horses were the first of the domesticated animals to be castrated by man. Horses were first caught and used as beasts of burden about eight thousand years ago in a region now called Iraq. Very soon they were used in warfare, when it was a positive advantage to be riding a furious, fighting stallion, but for other purposes a quiet, sensible beast was needed – for meat and transport, for example. There must have been a concern about lack of breeding animals at one point as the Islamic culture actually banned the castration of horses on religious grounds.

The methods used for castrating equines have changed very little in essential details over the centuries. A study of Roman and Arabic texts proves this very readily. Basically the animal had to be restrained in such a way as to enable the operator to make two incisions into the scrotum and remove both testicles. Not only that but a method of stopping the blood flow had to be used also or the animal would bleed to death. The Romans learned from the Greeks, who learned in turn from the Arabs that the easiest, safest way to achieve this was to cast the horse with ropes and then tie its legs to avoid it injuring itself or the human surgeon.

As a young vet newly into practice I found the method my colleagues used to castrate horses to be very old fashioned, but it was safe and very effective. The animal was restrained with a nose twitch and then given a sedative injection into the jugular vein. This usually worked quite quickly, which made it easier for the vet to inject local anaesthetic into the scrotal area. Then came the dangerous bit! The operation starts with the horse standing and the vet crouched half under the animal's belly with scalpel in hand, ready to make the necessary incisions. It is not difficult to imagine what a difficult and dangerous position this is for the surgeon. Many patients – even well sedated and with local anaesthetic in place – would still react violently to the first cut. No vet I knew ever wore protective clothing or a hard hat. It was usually 'take a deep breath and hope that no one was going to get hurt by flying hooves'.

With the incisions made, clams were used to stop any bleeding. These were two pieces of wood around four to five inches long and about the thickness of a middle finger, held together at one end by boiled string. The inner surface had a caustic ointment on it, known as red blister. The clams were placed on either side of the exposed blood vessels and a small leather collar, to give a tourniquet effect, closed the ends that were not held by the string. The horse was then left like this for twenty-four hours, with the testicles hanging free under the animal's belly and exposed to the elements. The animal was revisited next day and the now dried out testicles were removed without any risk of bleeding. It was a highly successful procedure, which had – with the obvious refinements of sedative and local anaesthetic injections – been in use for many centuries. The Romans and Arabs used clams to stop bleeding but did not have the chemical aids to allow them to do the operation with the animal upright.

In more modern times horses are still castrated while they are standing by vets who have universally abandoned clams for an instrument called an emasculator. This, after the initial incision is made, removes the testicles with a crushing action on the blood vessels that stops heavy bleeding. Otherwise the operation is the same as described for using the clams. It still leaves ample opportunity for the patient to bite back by inflicting collateral damage on the vet and his or her helpers.

In common with many other vets I rather quickly abandoned the sedative and local route for castrations in favour of giving my patients a full general anaesthetic. This renders the patient unconscious and has them lying on the ground. It makes it possible for the surgical site to be cleaned properly and the operation to be carried out unhurriedly with far less risk to the surgeon and the horse. The blood vessels are ligated with an absorbable material such as catgut, and before the horse is awakened from its slumbers the surgical area is dusted with a wound dressing and fly-repellent powder.

The anaesthetic I used to use for such operations was originally developed for use in dart guns, for immobilising wild animals such as elephants. It is highly dangerous stuff for the vet and nurses to be handling but not for the animal. Very great care had to be taken when handling the chemical not to spill any on human skin and the vet had to avoid an accidental injection at all costs.

Vets have died after accidents with this drug. For this very reason I always took a veterinary nurse with me and she had the antidote ready in case of trouble. All of my nurses were trained in how to administer the antidote, but given all the possible administration sites on the human body, not one of them will tell me their chosen place on me should such an emergency arise.

The advantage of using this potentially dangerous drug is that it is very safe in horses and they will not come round from the anaesthetic until they are given the antidote. This, when given into the vein, will have them on their feet and eating within two to three minutes. Never the less it's always a relief when the patient is awake, on his feet, the operation complete and everybody well.

After one operation was finished and the pony had just got to its feet, it blundered around a bit and knocked into my nurse Janet and sent her flying. I helped her to her feet, fearing the worst as she had gone a very nasty grey colour.

She was in shock! She had landed in a very liquid dung heap, bottom first! Much of it was still stuck to her rear end. I did offer to scrape as much off as possible – but she declined. She had to sit on newspaper and suffer all the car windows wide open all the way back to the surgery. It quite made up for all the threats of where she would inject any antidote into me – if the need arose.

As I have said, my equine patients are asleep and lying on the ground while I operate on them, but it is often quite difficult to find a suitable soft piece of earth on which to drop the horse. On one occasion I met a client and his horse at a location of his choice. It was the end of a narrow lane where he said there was a good site for the procedure. As I followed him and his horse along the lane carrying all my required kit I soon realised where he meant. It was the local golf course and neither he nor I were members, although I couldn't answer for the horse. The ground beside the third tee was perfect and the fairway was deserted. The operation went like clockwork, with no hitches and fortunately no spectators. I did heave a huge sigh of relief when it was all over but afterwards I realised I could always boast to golfing clients that I had taken two off on that particular par four hole without them really knowing what I was talking about.

Castrating sheep and cattle is a much easier procedure for all concerned – not least the patient. The easiest method is to apply a tight rubber ring around the neck of the scrotum. It causes the whole of the scrotum to slough off after a few days and there is very little risk to the patient, and no blood. This has to be done in the first seven days of life. After that age it is not allowed as the procedure may be too painful and is banned on welfare grounds. Farmers and stockmen like to use the rubber ring method, as it is quick and simple, unlike the operation that many farmers used to employ.

Some farmers in Scotland, and my father was one of them, used to castrate ram lambs with their teeth. My father used this technique every year and, what's more, it was a method that made some sense. The lambs were held with their legs restrained and their backsides sitting on the top rail of the sheep fold, belly towards the surgeon. The farmer would make two quick cuts with a very sharp knife and then extract the testicles with his teeth. It was done in this way as invariably the shepherd's or farmer's mouth was much cleaner than his hands, which considerably reduced the risk of infection to the sheep.

I used to have a gym teacher who made my life and several of my friends' lives miserable. He was a bully and he would pester me to take him a bag of lambs' testicles when he knew the lambs were being castrated. He liked them fried, he said. The sheep helped me bite back at him and have my secret revenge as he had no idea how the job was done.

Dad carried on this way with the sheep for many years and only stopped when he had to have dentures. He just couldn't do the job without his own teeth and had to use the rubber ring method thereafter.

Otherwise sheep are not noted for being able to bite back or retaliate against a human tormentor, although some rams or tups do occasionally have their moments. In my final year of being a vet student, we the students were gathered outside a field with a lecturer, looking at some rather fine Charolais rams. Most of us knew they had a certain reputation for being feisty, but one of our number did not. He should have done as he, in another life, had been a sheep farmer and thought he knew a thing or two about sheep. He was being a bit pedantic with the lecturer, who was getting fed up with him so he asked Pat if he would mind just going into the field and bringing the sheep nearer so we could all get a better look at them. It was a bit cruel really but the rams – all six of them – were not about to be moved and proceeded to charge at Pat with malicious intent. We all fell over ourselves laughing at him as he tried to get out of the paddock with some semblance of dignity. He never again tried to impress his fellow students with his knowledge of sheep.

Cattle have to be handled with care. They can grow to a considerable size and weight and if an individual beast wants to make life difficult for a human handler it can very easily. Cattle can and do kick with their hind feet and will attack with their heads and butt if really annoyed. A head butt, if the animal still has horns, can kill not only people, but I have known a bull to kill a lovely Arab mare with a horn hooked into her rib cage. One of my former partners, Elaine, was nearly killed by an enraged cow that had just given birth and was protecting her calf against all strangers. She was knocked over and trampled on and for a few moments it was thought she had broken her back. It left her with chronic pain and it was not long after that she decided to stop farm animal work. Some accidents happen when least expected and in the most seemingly innocuous way and farmer themselves – even the most experienced – are not immune to being hurt either.

A few summer evenings ago I was attending to a heifer that was having calving difficulties. The beast was frightened and she was being difficult, but I eventually got a rope and then a halter on her. John, the farmer, and I got her tied up to fence railing and I commenced my examination. She twisted away from me and quite casually, with her big backside knocked John into the fence. There was quite an audible crack, which I thought was the fence spar breaking, only to realise a moment later that it was John's right arm that had caused the noise as the humerus bone snapped into two parts.

He slumped to the ground in agony and all thought for the heifer had to be forgotten for the moment.

It was some time before an ambulance arrived and John was in so much pain that he begged me to give him a painkiller out of my large animal bag. I resisted the temptation as it could have compromised any further treatment he was going to need, but it wasn't easy to hear him in pain, knowing I had the drugs in my bag which would have made him feel more comfortable. I limited my assistance to putting his arm in a sling and mopping his brow until professional medical help arrived. By the time he was packed off to hospital, we were in total darkness and the heifer still required attention.

It was just as well for her sake that on examination I found the she wasn't quite ready to give birth. I injected her to delay the onset of second stage labour until it was daylight. I went back to the farm at six in the morning with my daughter Kate and delivered with some difficulty a fine bull calf. I think it was some consolation to John, lying in his 'bed of pain' in hospital, that at least we got a live calf and it had all been worthwhile in the end, even if he couldn't be there at the birth. I still think the cow got the best of the encounter.

Animals in good health are hearty eaters and seem to derive much pleasure from munching and digesting their food. Livestock farming in the Fens has been in decline for years despite the presence of a lot of waste vegetable material, which can be used for feeding and fattening cattle. Potatoes that have been rejected by the supermarkets as not marketable taste just as good to a hungry bullock as a perfectly shaped one, and are very cheap to buy. However, feeding raw potatoes to cattle can cause health problems due to gluttony. Bullocks eating potatoes are very prone to being in competition with their neighbour to see who can eat the most. This can result in a half-chewed potato being swallowed hurriedly and the tuber then blocks the gullet. When this happens the animal's life is at once put at risk. The clinical picture is alarming. The distracted beast looks an image of misery. It coughs, gags and drools copious amounts of saliva, which it cannot swallow due to the obstruction. The animal's abdomen begins to swell up quickly with gas as a result of the blockage preventing its release. Under normal circumstances, this gas that is produced as part of the normal digestive process is belched up by the bovine every few minutes. If these gases – and they are mostly methane – are not released within a fairly short period of time, then the bullock will die in great distress with circulatory and heart failure.

For a time it was the most common emergency job during the winter months, when the farmers were feeding potatoes, carrots or parsnips. The usual call over the radio was, 'Can you go to Mick Crowson's as soon as possible? He has a potato stuck.' Of course they meant Mr Crowson had a bullock being choked by a potato, but I got the message.

On arriving at the scene, if I was lucky Mick would have the animal restrained within a cattle crush. If not, the first job was to get the beast behind a gate, where it might be possible to hold and examine it.

Then I had to assess where the obstruction might be. If it was not too far down the throat it was sometimes possible to put a hand and an arm in, grasp the object and pull it out. It sounds easy but believe me it is not. Even with a gag in the mouth to keep it open it feels as if your hand and arm are in a mincing machine, and the last time I used this method my right arm finished up looking like a raw, red sausage.

If the obstruction is further down the neck, or even in the chest, the next approach is to push the potato further down the gullet and into the stomach. An instrument called a probang is used for this method of treatment, and it is a semi-rigid tube, like a stomach tube but with a stiff rod down the centre. These tubes used to have brass at both ends and had a leather casing, but more modern types are made out of plastic, which if anything works better and is not so dangerous to the beast.

The animal's head is held firmly by the left arm and hand. This procedure is greatly helped if you are built like Geoff Capes. Then the right hand passes the instrument down the throat until it touches the obstruction. Gentle pressure is applied, and in most of the cases the potato is moved into the stomach, where it is easily digested. The stomach gases are released and the bullock is instantly out of danger.

These gases stink dreadfully, and having been within range on many occasions has made me much more tolerant of human 'garlic breath'.

There are still times when despite everything the obstruction will not be moved and it is imperative to let the gases out as quickly as possible to save the animal's life. Now is the time for the trocar and cannula. This is a fiendish looking piece of equipment, a bit like a rocket-shaped dagger. It is inserted through a skin incision on the left flank of the animal and then pushed further into the cow's stomach. At this point the trocar is withdrawn, leaving the cannula behind as a tube through which the stomach gases escape. The relief again to the patient is instant and immense. Animals on the point of death will suddenly stop dying, and within seconds will look almost back to normal.

The gas which escapes is mostly methane, and I have often felt tempted in the euphoria of the moment to put a light to the gas as it escapes, just for the pyrotechnic effect. Often tempted but never foolish enough to try it, as I believe a German vet once did. The flames set fire to a barn and burned it and its contents to the ground. What happened to the patient I do not know, but I was told the vet was sued successfully for a large sum of money.

Having let the gases escape from the stomach, and made the animal safe, you must not forget about the potato that is still there blocking the gullet. While it is still in situ the animal cannot eat or drink, but fortunately Mother Nature comes to the rescue most of the time. Usually saliva from the mouth causes the potato to partially digest and soften within twenty-four hours, and it is then swallowed or successfully pushed down with the probang. When it is in the stomach, then and only then is it safe to remove the cannula.

Not all cases of bloat are the result of stomach obstructions. There can be many different reasons, but by far the most common after a gullet obstruction is frothy bloat. Gas is suspended in the stomach liquid to form a froth, which can again result in the death of the animal due to over-distension of the stomach. The treatment is fairly straightforward and does not require much in the way of heroics by the vet or farmer. It just needs the patient to be dosed with a vegetable oil to break up the froth into gas and liquid, and the patient then burps up the gas in the normal way. The only hazard for the operator is the vegetable oil that often escapes from the drenching bottle during the process and very messily tends to run down the arm.

Some animals will have a tendency to bloat frequently for reasons known only to themselves, and when this happens I will operate and make a permanent hole, called a fistula, in the bullock's side. This allows gas to freely pass out into the atmosphere and the bullock will never be at risk of dying from bloat. They also tend to put on weight really well, as they never feel full. You have to be careful how you approach an animal that has a fistula, as coming from the left side it is all too easy to be suddenly enveloped in stomach contents if the beast coughs. I am sure they do it on purpose sometimes.

Being around cattle can be a hazardous, messy, smelly business when they are ill, which much of the time is due to what they are being fed and is not the animals' fault. The worst smell I ever encountered in a cattle pen was when the farmer was feeding onions. The atmosphere was tainted for hundreds of yards around the farm and it wasn't the beasts' fault! They will eat whatever is put in front of them, and if the consequences are a bit of diarrhoea and bad breath it gives the animals an extra weapon. There are few things more inclined to upset a visiting vet than having a wet 'shitty' tail being swished in his face a few times.

You might be forgiven for thinking that working with large animals carries more risk to life and limb than caring for pets. This I have to say is not my experience as I have had more bites than kicks in my time. Treating and handling any animal can be risky as a patient is often frightened and in pain. Seeing a dog or a cat in the surgery puts them at a disadvantage as they are not in their own territory and they will often behave themselves better than they would if they were at home with their owners.

I had a good example of this many years ago when I was called to a house where the family Labrador was reputed to be in some pain and required attention. The family could not bring him to the surgery as they said he was in so much pain they could not get him in the car.

I knew the owners quite well and was received most warmly when I arrived. The dog was in the back garden and so, accompanied by the husband and wife, out I went to see the patient. I knew from previous encounters with the dog that his temperament was not the best but I was not expecting too much in the way of trouble.

On seeing the deputation, Ben, helpful as ever, took himself off to the bottom of the garden and refused all commands to come back. Instead of going to get him and putting him on a lead, the master of the household suggested that Ben might come back if he was bribed with a dish of milk – his absolute favourite. I should have vetoed this immediately but I took the line of least resistance and agreed to the proposal.

The milk was produced without delay and had the desired effect. Ben arrived to seek his reward for 'being a good boy.' I don't think so! In my dreams!

I should have heard even more alarm bells ring when the owner suggested that as soon as Ben settled to drink the milk, I was to walk up behind him and drop the leash over the dog's head.

I approached from behind as planned and got within two yards of the animal when he turned round and – without a moment's hesitation – launched himself straight at my throat. He was a nightmare vision of bared white teeth, dripping milk and hatred-filled, yellow eyes. He thought, I'm sure, that I was about to remove the milk and he wasn't going to let that happen. Self-preservation, not having time to do anything else, made me stick out my hands and arms to fend him off and I found myself catching him in mid-flight on his route towards my neck. I was left holding him at arm's length with my hands on either side of his collar. We tumbled over, bowled by the impetus of his attack, and continued our struggle on the lawn.

He was doing his damnedest to get me and I, for my part, having lost all sense of dignity, was just intent on self-preservation of my own.

I looked around desperate for assistance, only to find that both husband and wife had mysteriously disappeared. After what seemed like an eternity but must, I suppose, have only been a few seconds, Ben seemed to come to whatever sense he had left. He broke off his attack and disappeared into the shrubbery.

It took a few moments to recover, and after a cup of restorative coffee I suggested the examination be put off for another day. I thought if he was fit enough to attack me, then he could wait for another twenty-four hours until he calmed down. He was brought around to the surgery next morning suitably sedated and muzzled and he was no more trouble. He was suffering from a bit of arthritis, for which as yet there is no cure, but I could make him feel better with some anti-inflammatory painkillers. They may even have improved his temper. As for the attack, it was entirely my own fault as I should have foreseen the likely sequence of events and had nobody but myself to blame.

I learned a lot from that joyless encounter with Ben and have never from that time been bitten by a dog that I knew had a suspect temperament. That doesn't mean I haven't been bitten since then, as you can never totally guard against the unexpected. Most owners are very good about warning you if their dog is bad tempered or downright nasty but there are some that can take a perverse pleasure in seeing the vet getting bitten. I have up until now resisted the temptation of adding a bit more onto the bill for wear and tear and medical attention but I'm not sure I will always hold out. It's not that you can get any redress from the patient but I did have one occasion when a clinical decision made me feel a lot better after a bite!

It was a pretty miserable winter morning and I was standing somewhat wearily on the doorstep of a house in Wisbech, having just knocked on the door. The door opened and I was just half way through my opening of, 'Good morning, how are you, I'm the vet,' when a rather massive, hairy German Shepherd dog came hurtling around the corner of the house and grabbed my thigh in an all embracing, teeth clenching (both his and mine) jaw lock! I leapt forward, emitting something between a high pitched scream and a falsetto giggle.

'My heck,' said the lady at the door, 'I told you, Dad to hold on to him!' Dad was the husband who arrived just too late to witness the altercation but was holding an empty lead by way of explanation.

With the ensuing noise and confusion, 'Sabre', the cause of all the trouble, took the opportunity to slip away unnoticed, while I did my best to restore some sanity to the situation.

'Are you all right young man?' said Dad, stifling a grin with difficulty, as the world knows there is nothing funnier than the vet getting bitten. It's like one more victory for the underdog or even a comment on our fee structure.

I leant against the doorframe and could feel a warm liquid trickling down my leg. 'Relax,' I said to myself, 'it's only blood.' I put my hand down the back of my trouser leg and was relieved to find only the holes where the teeth went through and no tearing of material. The trousers were more or less intact.

The good lady, showing more concern than her husband, offered me the use of the bathroom to further examine the state of my injuries, but I remembered the advice from my student days, 'never show pain,' and turned the offer down, but with thanks.

Instead I turned my attention to the patient, who was soon found hiding under the kitchen table. Dad, who had reunited the dog with the lead, soon dragged out the reluctant Sabre from under the table. He was immediately restrained and muzzled and presented for examination. It didn't take too long to discover the cause of the dog's bad temper. He had an all too apparent lump on his bottom, which was very easy to diagnose. It was a cancerous growth called an anal adenoma. The best treatment for the dog was an operation to remove the mass, and as soon as possible as it was getting rather large and was bleeding intermittently.

As part of the operation, as well as removal of the lump, it is advisable to castrate the dog at the same time. This is to try and prevent the tumour from regrowing after it has been removed, as the growth is hormone dependent.

I thought the case over for a few moments and talked to the owners as to how to treat Sabre. I hope that only clinical considerations came to mind, but my ultimate decision on the dog's treatment eased the throbbing on my leg considerably.

I am often asked if I have ever been frightened by an animal and I have to say I have not been – apprehensive, yes; frightened, no. For a vet to be frightened would mean he or she would not be able to do the job properly. I have been badly frightened just once in the surgery but not by an animal.

I was treating a cat for a routine complaint – I think it was an abscess – and at the end of the consultation the lady owner, to whom I will admit I paid very little attention, pressed an envelope into my hand and said it was very private and for my eyes only.

I scuttled off into the office, leaving her at the desk paying the bill. I slit open the letter hoping for something like a ten-pound tip, only to find a written note instead. It was a proposal of marriage! I swear I had never seen the lady before. She was middle-aged and very pleasant and I am sure she must have mistaken me for someone else. I didn't have a clue what to do and in the end I did what any red-blooded male would have done in similar circumstances. I hid. I stayed in the office until the other members of staff assured me that she had left the building. I never saw her again but I worried for quite a long time afterwards that she was going to come back and get me!

CHAPTER 14

At The End of The Year

DECEMBER IS A RATHER strange month in the veterinary calendar. There are times when the surgeries are very quiet, when everybody is too busy shopping for Christmas and too hard pressed for cash, so that pets' problems or routine operations are pushed to one side and forgotten for the moment. On other days, and it is often nearer to the bank holiday, the waiting room is crammed full to overflowing with animals and clients who have decided that they really must get their dog's anal glands emptied before the long Christmas break.

In the large animal practice we tend not to see quite the same effect as farmers will only call out the vet when it is really necessary, and are not too fussy whether it is Christmas or not. I always tend to associate Christmas time with lambing and newborn lambs. This might seem a bit strange as nature usually arranges for lambs to be born in the Spring, when it is a bit warmer, and not in the depths of winter. There is however, at Easter time a demand for English lamb, which cannot be met by lambs being born in March or April. For some years now it has been possible to meet the demand for lamb in the supermarket by inducing ewes to come into season early. There are a variety of clever ways to make this happen.

A simple method of doing this is to introduce a vasectomised tup into the flock of ewes in September. These animals are known as teasers for obvious reasons. Their presence stimulates the ewes into an early season without getting them pregnant. Once the ewes are all coming into season at the same time the vasectomised tup is removed from the field and the fertile ram is introduced instead. This has the effect of the ewes producing lambs early and all within a few days of each other.

Rams that are not suitable for breeding can have a vasectomy operation at a fairly early age and then can be used for years as teasers. One particular ram I performed this operation on turned out to be a magnificent animal with a very fine set of horns. He was called 'Big Business' and he lorded it over his flock every year with significant pride. I'm sure he would have been mortified if he knew he was only firing blanks.

This teaser system is particularly successful and cheap. A vasectomised tup will outlive, and work much longer than, a normal ram, and by using them the farmer is able to get ewes to lamb in late February or early March. To get lambs to be born around Christmas, hormone treatment has to be used. The very early trials for the hormone treatment of sheep to produce early lambs were carried out on upland farms in Scotland and the farm at home was used in the early pioneering work. Right from the start the treatment was very successful. Hormone impregnated sponges were inserted into the vagina of each ewe about six weeks before the normal breeding season. These were left in situ for up to fourteen days, and a hormone derived from pregnant mares is also injected. The sheep have a normal season when the sponges are removed. If they are then served by a fertile ram and if the shepherd has got his dates correct, the first lambs will be born around Christmas.

The last few weeks of gestation can be a hazardous time for a ewe. There is the risk of abortion due to infectious agents, which is an all too common problem. The main hazard to sheep and the unborn is, however, the result of bad management and incorrect feeding. It is increasingly common these days for ewes to give birth, if not indoors at least in large enclosed yards. This has proved to be a great blessing to man and beast alike as no one can tell me there is any intrinsic value in freezing on a hillside or a Fenland field while giving birth or while attending a parturient ewe, especially in December or January.

This practice does however have its hazards due to a condition called Pregnancy Toxaemia. Management and feeding has to be very accurate in the last four weeks of pregnancy. If the shepherd gets it wrong the consequences for both mother and the unborn can be disastrous. If you feed a sheep too well in early pregnancy, it will become too fat and by the time it needs extra energy from the diet in late pregnancy the animal may not be able to eat enough for its requirements. The sheep attempts to make up for this deficit by converting the body fat into energy. This unfortunately does not work too well as the fat is converted into ketones, which poison the sheep's metabolic systems. The answer to this difficulty, and it is sometimes difficult to get the balance right, is to start the animal on a low level of nutrition and build it up slowly during the pregnancy. When the mother-to-be is in the last six weeks of gestation it is then more possible for her to eat and digest enough food for herself and her unborn lambs without depleting her reserves. Exercise too is all-important in keeping the ewes healthy.

A few years ago now a client decided after years of trouble-free lambing out of doors, to house her in-lamb ewes in the run up to lambing. She brought them in from a freezing cold field and housed them in a cosy straw-filled yard. It was a disaster! Within a few days she had a big problem with her ewes. Many became extremely ill due to Pregnancy Toxaemia as the sheep's energy demands had completely changed. The very sick were difficult to treat. Oral drenches of glucose solutions were the order of the day – and night – and the worst affected were given intravenous drips. Despite intensive treatment two of the sheep died and others had to be aborted early to save their lives. All the others in the group, the mildly affected and the healthy ones as well, had to go out for a walk twice daily as the exercise seemed to have real value in preventing any more going down with the condition. Needless to say the animals themselves were quite disgusted by the whole idea, and of course couldn't see the point at all. I'm not even sure the farmer was totally convinced either but I'm sure it saved lives.

I was reminded at the time of an old-fashioned remedy, which I learned from my father and was tempted to try again. This was to provide the sheep with troughs of treacle or crude molasses. Sheep love treacle and it is a very good source of energy, and Dad never had any more trouble with Toxaemia after he hit on this idea. He did have to learn to take the troughs away after the sheep had lambed as lambs were forever getting stuck in the stuff, and sadly one year a lamb became so enmeshed in the sticky stuff that it died.

One of the more trying aspects of the Festive Season is having to turn down so many kind invitations. Wherever you go there always seems to be a party going on, which you are often invited to join and partake in a little of the festive cheer. These days with everyone so aware of the perils of drinking and driving, this cheer has to be confined to consuming the odd mince pie or Christmas cake with a cup of coffee. It wasn't always like that as I can remember all too well.

The first Christmas I had in the Fens I was called to a farm to a ewe with lambing difficulties. It was quite biblical in the straw filled yard under a clear, frosty sky. The shepherdess lived in a gypsy caravan in the yard so that she could be close to her pregnant mums, and it was a warm place to go, clean up and thaw out after having to strip down to lamb the ewe. All was well and two healthy lambs were produced to everyone's satisfaction. The farmer arrived just as I was packing up and invited me up to the 'big house' where a party was in full swing. It would have been churlish of me to refuse. I spent a convivial hour singing carols around the Christmas tree and drinking warm punch before disappearing into the night on my next call.

One of the best friends I have ever made I got to know very well after another Christmas night under the stars. Mike was a sheep farmer and called me to a ewe about two o'clock in the morning. It was again a bright, clear, moonlit night with more than a touch of frost in the air – in fact it was freezing hard.

The expectant mum was in a pen in the lambing yard and we attended to her with a brisk efficiency and, considering it was the middle of the night, commendable good humour. The ewe had a minor presentational problem with her lambs in that they both wanted to be born at the same time. It was merely a matter of pushing one back and sorting out which leg belonged to which lamb. Once this was done the ewe almost managed the rest for herself.

Afterwards in the barn, as I was washing my hands in the bucket of warm water, I noticed that Mike, the farmer, had a bottle of malt whisky in the opened feed bin. Out of somewhere he conjured up two fairly clean glasses and I sat on a feed bag and gave my considered opinion as to the quality of his whisky. It was excellent but it took some time and a lot of discussion to consider properly as it was a serious matter. We adjourned to the house for greater comfort and the talk developed into other philosophical matters. Two hours passed as if in a moment and I suddenly realised to my horror that it was nearly four in the morning and I hadn't left a note as to where I was or what I was doing! I rushed off home praying there hadn't been another call and my wife wasn't waiting up worrying where I was, and whether I had had an accident. It was long before the days of the mobile phone.

I needn't have worried, as when I arrived home smelling like a distillery she was still sound asleep and blissfully unaware of my nocturnal misdemeanours. Only the dogs were pleased to see me. I had made a ewe comfortable, saved two lambs' lives and made a life long friend that Christmas night. But it is not a performance I would dare to repeat today. Except I still do enjoy his whisky – and he mine – but I now don't drive afterwards.

Patients that refuse to get better despite all the best of modern medicine are a nuisance at the best of times but when it happens on Christmas Day itself it can be very trying indeed. Colic in horses is an ever-present threat and horse owners are terrified that their animal might get colic, develop a twisted gut and have to be put down. Colic can happen at any time, it is usually feed related and the word just means stomach pain. Symptoms can appear at any hour of the day or night and for a number of different reasons but the most common cause is constipation. This mostly is the result of eating unsuitable food such as straw bedding, and relieving chronic constipation in a horse can often be a bit of a marathon performance.

One particular mare became very ill on Christmas morning. She was very constipated and in a lot of pain. What made matters worse was her owner was away for the Christmas break and the friend who was looking after the horse was feeling very guilty as she thought that she was responsible for the mare's condition and was doom laded. When I arrived for my first visit of the day the locum was already predicting the imminent demise of the animal and trying to work out how she was going to break the news to the owner.

The mare was very bunged up and I gave her a large dose of a pain-relieving drug and about a gallon of liquid paraffin by a stomach tube, which is a very slow process as it takes ages for the oil to pass down the tube. I revisited her four times that day and each time I had to give her more pain relief and more fluids by stomach tube. It wasn't much of a Christmas Day anyway. I was happily dodging family rows as to what should be the essential viewing item on the television – a John Wayne movie or ballet – and the washing up.

Boxing Day arrived to find the mare had finally succeeded in clearing herself and there was a satisfying pile of dung in the corner of the stable and a further mess half way up the wall. She was happily munching on some hay and the smile on her keeper's face said that the epitaphs had been discarded for another time and place.

Sad moments happen all too frequently as well, whether it is Christmas or not. One of the worst happened about ten years ago on Christmas night. The patient was a tiny heifer that should never have been pregnant and she had a very large, dead calf inside her. It was a night of freezing fog and after an initial examination I was sure that to remove her calf was going to take many hours of hard labour. The only way to save the young cow, as the calf had been dead for many hours, was to dismember it while it was still in the womb and remove it in pieces. A caesarean operation would have been quicker but I felt that it would be more likely to cause the death of the heifer as the uterus was grossly infected and a fatal peritonitis would have been the likely outcome. The alternative to the caesarean, the embryotomy procedure is conducted through the vagina. Various fiendish looking instruments, including cutting wire which is like thick cheese wire, are used to remove the limbs and other body parts until the foetus is reduced enough in size to remove it with the minimum amount of stress to the mother. It's a difficult, tiring, messy job at the best of times but that night, in that weather and being very aware of the trauma that the animal was suffering, everyone's Christmas spirit was at an all time low. The operation took from about nine in the evening until nearly one in the morning and I have rarely felt so tired and so fed up after a job. The heifer survived the experience but only just and was never fit to breed from again.

When the emergency phone rings over the Christmas period it does not automatically mean an emergency visit has to be made. Much of the time a friendly word of advice is all that is required. I still laugh when I recall a frantic phone call I received one Christmas Eve. It was from a lady who was in a bit of a panic. She, like most hostesses, had been rushing around trying to make dinner before guests arrived and had developed a bit of a headache. She was in too much of a hurry, went to the cupboard and, without checking the label on the bottle, swallowed two cat worming pills, mistaking them for paracetamol. When she realised her mistake she was horrified as she remembered the last time she had given one to the cat, it had rushed out to the garden to dig a hole to relieve itself. It had caused instant diarrhoea!

The poor woman was more than a little concerned that the same fate awaited her. She was very relieved (I use the word advisedly) when I assured her that she should be all right and that the dinner party would not be ruined by the hostess having to disappear at regular intervals.

Barry didn't call me very often, but when he did it usually meant trouble with a capital T. He called me one Christmas afternoon just after the Queen's Speech and asked me to visit.

He said he had a problem with his horse – it could not pass urine. This is not his exactly what he said but that was what he meant.

I knew my client. I knew very well I was usually the port of last resort and he would have tried many home made remedies before he felt justified in calling the 'vitnry.'

'What have you given it already?' I asked.

'Nothing – not a lot,' was the defensive reply, which was not like him at all.

'I don't believe you. You must have done.'

'Well I did stick an onion up its backside,' came the eventual, grudging reply.

'Why on earth did you did that?' was all I could think of to say.

The scorn in his voice was obvious. 'Well everyone knows,' he said, 'that's the best way to make a horse have a pee and it hasn't had a pee for over a day now. What else could I do?' he demanded to know.

Well as a technique it was all news to me, but for the horse's sake I thought I ought, even although it was Christmas Day and I had indigestion, to go along and have a look.

The patient was a good looking two-year old piebald colt. He looked very uncomfortable and was pawing at the straw in the stable and repeatedly getting up and down. It looked like a typical case of colic and again constipation seemed to be the cause of the abdominal pain. The onion, positioned where it was, seemed to me to be doing very little to alleviate the situation.

My first job after assessing the animal was to remove the offending vegetable. As I was doing this the animal got such a fright – well, it was the second time that day he had had a hand and arm stuck up his bottom – that when the onion came out so did everything else and the constipation was released in one rather massive dollop. And most of it went over me.

I turned around to remonstrate with Barry and tell him what

a fool I thought he was, only to see him in a heap in the corner of the box, shaking quietly.

Was it an alcoholic convulsion, as he had obviously had a few pints of the amber liquid? Was it heck! He was having a good laugh at my expense, and when I turned back to look at my patient I had to join in, as there was the animal standing passing urine – for the first time in twenty-four hours. It did little good to tell Barry that withholding urine was one of the classical symptoms of colic in a horse. To his dying day he was still convinced as to the efficacy of his treatment.

'You just have to give it time to work – vitnry.'

This working vitnry took time to help Barry to his feet and went home to what was left over from Christmas for another year.

The Quest for the Original Horse Whisperers

Russell Lyon

ISBN 1 84282 020 6 HB £16.99

Who were the Original Horse Whisperers? What was the Secret Society of Horsemen?

The book tells the story of the Secret Society of Horsemen who were the Original Horse Whisperers. The Societies were formed originally in the North East of Scotland about two hundred years ago but spread rapidly throughout Scotland and then in to East Anglia and across to the United States. The roots of the Society are obscure but many of the customs and oaths may go back to pagan times. The ploughmen who formed these groups came to exploit their membership much like a primitive trade union and used their membership to improve their conditions on the farm.

New members of the Society were told a secret 'magic' word under severe oath of silence which when whispered in the horses ear gave each new horseman immediate and total control over his horse. Russell Lyon investigates this "Word" and the mythology behind it and reveals the secret knowledge that the horsemen who were the Original Whisperers used to make their horses obey their master's command – instantly and without hesitation.

What were the secret oaths and rituals that all new recruits had to undertake to become members of the Secret Society?

How could a Word whispered in the ear of a horse weighing at least 500kg make it obey a man who weighed at best no more than 75kg?

How different are the Original Whisperers of two hundred years ago to Modern Whisperers?

Were they better? Could their methods be used today?

Robert Redford's acclaimed film *The Horse Whisperer*, based on the best-selling novel by Nicholas Evans, heightened curiosity in modern day 'Horse Whisperers', such as American Monty Roberts.

Foxes: the Blood is Wild

Bridget MacCaskill

ISBN 0 946487 71 5 PBK £9.99

A 'must' for those who respect and care for foxes!

WILDLIFE GUARDIAN

In the endless struggle between man and nature, Bridget and Don MacCaskill's Highland home has always been a haven for injured and orphaned wildlife, from red deer to wildcats. The fascinating story begins with the rescue of two near-starved fox cubs called Rufus and Rusty, victims of their species' vicious reputation, and charts their often amusing journey into adulthood under the watchful eye of their new human 'parents'. Along the way, they are regularly joined by other wild creatures in need of the MacCaskills' help – badgers, birds of prey and a majestic golden eagle among them.

The Blood is Wild is a dramatic yet touching, brilliantly observed account of the precarious existence of wildlife in the Highlands. It is written with the same fondness that was so infectious in the TV film and book On the Swirl of the Tide, the story about the survival of otters in the North of Scotland.

Their book has suspense, marvellous scenery and practical information... good armchair reading and more. Don's photographs are superb.

NAOMI LEWIS, EVENING STANDARD

The Blood is Wild is funny and moving... This wildlife epic will bring much joy to animal lovers. TODAY

Otters: On the Swirl of the Tide

Bridget MacCaskill

ISBN 0 946487 67 7 PBK £9.99

Otters have a strong appeal and deserve all the books they can get. No wonder the MacCaskills were enchanted. Nicholas Wollaston,

OBSERVER

The story of Bodach, Palethroat and Pinknose unfolded to Bridget and Don MacCaskill over a period of twelve patient years. Slowly, the wild otters became accustomed to the scent of the humans around their remote Highland sea loch, and the couple were able to observe the habits and behaviour of these beautiful creatures. Cubs are born and grow up with their parents, and the otters regularly encounter other animals, sometimes with amusing results. Whatever the event, Bridget and Don are there with pen and camera, ready to record the details.

On the Swirl of the Tide is a vivid and intimate portrait of the lives of otters in the wild, part of which was shared with the cameras for Central Television's Nature Watch series. The beautiful colour photographs from Don MacCaskill reveal details never before shown, and Bridget's sympathetic portrait of the lifestyle and behaviour of these wild creatures is the most enchanting and powerful account of otter life since Gavin Maxwell's bestseller A Ring of Bright Water. Whereas Maxwell's wonderful account primarily focuses on otters in a domestic setting, the otters in this book are truly wild.

A marvellous tale of adventures with otters... there is much beauty in the book.

EVERGREEN

Superb photographs. The opportunities to observe and photograph their feeding, grooming play, and mating in full daylight were unique.

ALAN BENNETT, DAILY TELEGRAPH

This book is sure to leave everybody wanting a second helping.

JOHN CRICHTON, SCOTTISH WILDLIFE

Men & Beasts: Wild Men and Tame Animals of Scotland

Poems and Prose by Valerie Gillies
Photographs by Rebecca Marr
ISBN 0 946487 92 8 PB £15.00

Come and meet some wild men and tame beasts. Explore the fleeting moment and capture the passing of time in these portrait studies which document a year's journey. Travel across Scotland with poet Valerie Gillies and photographer Rebecca Marr: share their passion for a land where wild men can sometimes be tamed and tame beasts can get really wild.

Among the wild men they find are a gunner in Edinburgh Castle, a Highland shepherd, a ferryman on the River Almond, an eel fisher on Loch Ness, a Borders fencer, and a beekeeper on a Lowland estate.

The beasts portrayed in their own settings include Clydesdale foals, Scottish deerhounds, Highland cattle, blackface sheep, falcons, lurchers, bees, pigs, cashmere goats, hens, cockerels, tame swans and transgenic lambs.

Photograph, poem and reportage – a unique take on Scotland today.

'*Goin aroon the Borders wi Valerie an' Rebecca did my reputation the world o good. It's no often they see us wi beautiful talented women, ye ken.*' WALTER ELLIOT, fencer and historian

'*These poems are rooted in the elemental world.*' ROBERT NYE, *reviewing The Chanter's Tune in The Times*

'*Valerie Gillies is one of the most original voices of the fertile avant-guarde Scottish poetry.*' MARCO FAZZINI, l'Arco, Italia

'*The work of Valerie Gillies and Rebecca Marr is the result of true collaboration based on insight, empathy and generosity.*' JULIE LAWSON, Studies in Photography

'*Rebecca Marr's photos never fall into the trap of mere illustration, but rather they show a very individual vision – creative interpretation rather than prosaic document.*' ROBIN GILLANDERS, photographer

Half the royalties genereated from the sale of this publication will go to Maggie's Centre for the care of cancer patients.

Red Sky at Night

John Barrington
ISBN 0 946487 60 X PBK £8.99

'*I read John Barrington's book with growing delight. This working shepherd writes beautifully about his animals, about the wildlife, trees and flowers which surround him at all times, and he paints an unforgettable picture of his glorious corner of Western Scotland. It is a lovely story of a rather wonderful life*'. JAMES HERRIOT

John Barrington is a shepherd to over 750 Blackface ewes who graze 2,000 acres of some of Britain's most beautiful hills overlooking the deep dark water of Loch Katrine in Perthshire. The yearly round of lambing, dipping, shearing and the sales is marvellously interwoven into the story of the glen, of Rob Roy in whose house John now lives, of curling when the ice is thick enough, and of sheep dog trials in the summer. Whether up to the hills or along the glen, John knows the haunts of the local wildlife: the wily hill fox, the grunting badger, the herds of red deer, and the shrews, voles and insects which scurry underfoot. He sets his seasonal clock by the passage of birds on the loch, and jealously guards over the golden eagle's eyrie in the hills. Paul Armstrong's sensitive illustrations are the perfect accompaniment to the evocative text.

'*Mr Barrington is a great pleasure to read. One learns more things about the countryside from this account of one year than from a decade of The Archers*'. THE DAILY TELEGRAPH

'*Powerful and evocative... a book which brings vividly to life the landscape, the wildlife, the farm animals and the people who inhabit John's vista. He makes it easy for the reader to fall in love with both his surrounds and his commune with nature*'. THE SCOTTISH FIELD

'*An excellent and informative book.... not only an account of a shepherd's year but also the diary of a naturalist. Little escapes Barrington's enquiring eye and, besides the life cycle of a sheep, he also gives those of every bird, beast, insect and plant that crosses his path, mixing their histories with descriptions of the geography, local history and folklore of his surroundings*'. TLS

'*The family life at Glengyle is wholesome, appealing and not without a touch of the Good Life. Many will envy Mr Barrington his fastness home as they cruise up Loch Katrine on the tourist steamer*'. THE FIELD

Milk Treading

Nick Smith

ISBN 1 84282 037 0 PB £6.99

Life isn't easy for Julius Kyle, a jaded crime hack with the *Post*. When he wakes up on a sand barge with his head full of grit he knows things have to change. But how fast they'll change he doesn't guess until his best friend Mick jumps to his death off a fifty foot bridge outside the *Post*'s window. Worst of all, he's a cat. That means keeping himself scrupulously clean, defending his territory and battling an addiction to milk. He lives in Bast, a sprawling city of alleyways and claw-shaped towers... join Julius as he prowls deep into the crooked underworld of Bast, contending with political intrigue, territorial disputes and dog-burglars, murder, mystery and mayhem.

This is certainly the only cat-centred political thriller that I've read and it has a weird charm, not to mention considerable humour...
AL KENNEDY

A trip into a surreal and richly-realised feline-canine world.
ELLEN GALFORD

Milk Treading is equal parts Watership Down, Animal Farm, and The Big Sleep. A novel of class struggle, political intrigue and good old-fashioned murder and intrigue. And, oh yeah, all the characters are either cats or dogs.
TOD GOLDBERG, LAS VEGAS MERCURY

Smith writes with wit and energy creating a memorable brood of characters...
ALAN RADCLIFFE, THE LIST

The Kitty Killer Cult

Nick Smith

ISBN 1 84282 039 7 PBK £9.99
ISBN 1 84282 039 7 US $13.95

In the style of Raymond Chandler, this is hard-boiled detective fiction set in the city of Nub, where cats are king, killer and killed. Tiger Straight, PI, is past his prime, homeless and unemployed until the dame Connie Hant shows up. The PI is back, pawing the mean streets of Nub that he knows so well.

Straight has a new mission – to catch the killers of the broad's brothers. It leads him to the murky, tatty underbelly of Nub, throwing up more kitty deaths and a love for a certain make-up artiste. What are the links between these murders and will Straight and his bug loving side-kick Natasha survive to discover the answers before the edible Inspector Bix Mortis?

For those who know and love Smith's first novel, *Milk Treading*, this is the book feline crime hack Julius Kyle started to write.

'What this book so adequately expresses (in simple terms, of course) is that the Other, the enemy of which every animal is wary, exists within ourselves as well as beyond our molly-coddling environs. THE KITTY KILLER CULT *supports my own belief that we should one day be able to live in harmony with other species, offering them succour even as we learn from their alternate approaches to life.' The Professor in* MILK TREADING

'Nothing less than a disgrace,' was Bridget's opinion of the book in MILK TREADING*. 'The sort of narrow minded, anti-establishment liberal claptrap that leads to decadence and corruption. Now, I don't hold with the kind of sensationalist violence this author's previous books revel in, but at least they had simple, solid villains to teach youngsters a little patriotism.'*

Praise for MILK TREADING

'One of the most inventive novels to come out in years.' TOD GOLDBERG, LAS VEGAS MERCURY

Rum: Nature's Island

Magnus Magnusson

ISBN 0 946487 32 4 PBK £7.95

Rum: Nature's Island is the fascinating story of a Hebridean island from the earliest times through to the Clearances and its period as the sporting playground of a Lancashire industrial magnate, and on to its rebirth as a National Nature Reserve, a model for the active ecological management of Scotland's wild places.

Thoroughly researched and written in a lively accessible style, the book includes comprehensive coverage of the island's geology, animals and plants, and people, with a special chapter on the Edwardian extravaganza of Kinloch Castle. There is practical information for visitors to what was once known as 'the Forbidden Isle'; the book provides details of bothy and other accommodation, walks and nature trails. It closes with a positive vision for the island's future: biologically diverse, economically dynamic and ecologically sustainable.

Rum: Nature's Island is published in co-operation with Scottish Natural Heritage (of which Magnus Magnusson is Chairman) to mark the 40th anniversary of the acquisition of Rum by its predecessor, The Nature Conservancy.

Scotland, Land and People: An Inhabited Solitude:

James McCarthy

ISBN 0 946487 57 X PBK £7.99

'Scotland is the country above all others that I have seen, in which a man of imagination may carve out his own pleasures; there are so many inhabited solitudes.'

DOROTHY WORDSWORTH, in her journal of August 1803

An informed and thought-provoking profile of Scotland's unique landscapes and the impact of humans on what we see now and in the future. James McCarthy leads us through the many aspects of the land and the people who inhabit it: natural Scotland; the rocks beneath; land ownership; the use of resources; people and place; conserving Scotland's heritage and much more.

Written in a highly readable style, this concise volume offers an understanding of the land as a whole. Emphasising the uniqueness of the Scottish environment, the author explores the links between this and other aspects of our culture as a key element in rediscovering a modern sense of the Scottish identity and perception of nationhood.

'This book provides an engaging introduction to the mysteries of Scotland's people and landscapes. Difficult concepts are described in simple terms, providing the interested Scot or tourist with an invaluable overview of the country... It fills an important niche which, to my knowledge, is filled by no other publications.'

BETSY KING, Chief Executive, Scottish Environmental Education Council.

On the Trail of Robert Service

GW Lockhart

ISBN 0 946487 24 3 PBK £7.99

Robert Service is famed world-wide for his eye-witness verse-pictures of the Klondike goldrush. As a war poet, his work outsold Owen and Sassoon, and he went on to become the world's first million selling poet. In search of adventure and new experiences, he emigrated from Scotland to Canada in 1890 where he was caught up in the aftermath of the raging gold fever. His vivid dramatic verse bring to life the wild, larger than life characters of the gold rush Yukon, their bar-room brawls, their lust for gold, their trigger-happy gambles with life and love. 'The Shooting of Dan McGrew' is perhaps his most famous poem:

> A bunch of the boys were whooping it up in the Malamute saloon;
> The kid that handles the music box was hitting a ragtime tune;
> Back of the bar in a solo game, sat Dangerous Dan McGrew,
> And watching his luck was his light o'love, the lady that's known as Lou.

His storytelling powers have brought Robert Service enduring fame, particularly in North America and Scotland where he is something of a cult figure.

Starting in Scotland, *On the Trail of Robert Service* follows Service as he wanders through British Columbia, Oregon, California, Mexico, Cuba, Tahiti, Russia, Turkey and the Balkans, finally 'settling' in France.

This revised edition includes an expanded selection of illustrations of scenes from the Klondike as well as several photographs from the family of Robert Service on his travels around the world.

Wallace Lockhart, an expert on Scottish traditional folk music and dance, is the author of *Highland Balls & Village Halls* and *Fiddles & Folk*. His relish for a well-told tale in popular vernacular led him to fall in love with the verse of Robert Service and write his biography.

'*A fitting tribute to a remarkable man - a bank clerk who wanted to become a cowboy. It is hard to imagine a bank clerk writing such lines as:*
A bunch of boys were whooping it up...
The income from his writing actually exceeded his bank salary by a factor of five and he resigned to pursue a full time writing career.'
Charles Munn,
THE SCOTTISH BANKER

'*Robert Service claimed he wrote for those who wouldnit be seen dead reading poetry. His was an almost unbelievably mobile life... Lockhart hangs on breathlessly, enthusiastically unearthing clues to the poet's life.*' Ruth Thomas,
SCOTTISH BOOK COLLECTOR

'*This enthralling biography will delight Service lovers in both the Old World and the New.*'
Marilyn Wright,
SCOTS INDEPENDENT

On the Trail of John Muir

Cherry Good
ISBN 0 946487 62 6 PBK £7.99

Follow the man who made the US go green. Confidant of presidents, father of American National Parks, trailblazer of world conservation and voted a Man of the Millennium in the US, John Muir's life and work is of continuing relevance. A man ahead of his time who saw the wilderness he loved threatened by industrialisation and determined to protect it, a crusade in which he was largely successful. His love of the wilderness began at an early age and he was filled with wanderlust all his life.

Only by going in silence, without baggage, can on truly get into the heart of the wilderness. All other travel is mere dust and hotels and baggage and chatter. JOHN MUIR

Braving mosquitoes and black bears Cherry Good set herself on his trail – Dunbar, Scotland; Fountain Lake and Hickory Hill, Wisconsin; Yosemite Valley and the Sierra Nevada, California; the Grand Canyon, Arizona; Alaska; and Canada – to tell his story. John Muir was himself a prolific writer, and Good draws on his books, articles, letters and diaries to produce an account that is lively, intimate, humorous and anecdotal, and that provides refreshing new insights into the hero of world conservation.

John Muir chronology
General map plus 10 detailed maps covering the US, Canada and Scotland
Original colour photographs
Afterword advises on how to get involved
Conservation websites and addresses

Muir's importance has long been acknowledged in the US with over 200 sites of scenic beauty named after him. He was a Founder of The Sierra Club which now has over ¹⁄₂ million members. Due to the movement he started some 360 million acres of wilderness are now protected. This is a book which shows Muir not simply as a hero but as likeable humorous and self-effacing man of extraordinary vision.

'*I do hope that those who read this book will burn with the same enthusiasm for John Muir which the author shows.*'
WEST HIGHLAND FREE PRESS

On the Trail of William Wallace

David R. Ross
ISBN 0 946487 47 2 PBK £7.99

How close to reality was *Braveheart*?

Where was Wallace actually born?

What was the relationship between Wallace and Bruce?

Are there any surviving eye-witness accounts of Wallace?

How does Wallace influence the psyche of today's Scots?

On the Trail of William Wallace offers a refreshing insight into the life and heritage of the great Scots hero whose proud story is at the very heart of what it means to be Scottish. Not concentrating simply on the hard historical facts of Wallace's life, the book also takes into account the real significance of Wallace and his effect on the ordinary Scot through the ages, manifested in the many sites where his memory is marked.

In trying to piece together the jigsaw of the reality of Wallace's life, David Ross weaves a subtle flow of new information with his own observations. His engaging, thoughtful and at times amusing narrative reads with the ease of a historical novel, complete with all the intrigue, treachery and romance required to hold the attention of the casual reader and still entice the more knowledgable historian.

74 places to visit in Scotland and the north of England

One general map and 3 location maps

Stirling and Falkirk battle plans

Wallace's route through London

Chapter on Wallace connections in North America and elsewhere

Reproductions of rarely seen illustrations

On the Trail of William Wallace will be enjoyed by anyone with an interest in Scotland, from the passing tourist to the most fervent nationalist. It is an encyclopaedia-cum-guide book, literally stuffed with fascinating titbits not usually on offer in the conventional history book.

David Ross is organiser of and historical adviser to the Society of William Wallace.

'Historians seem to think all there is to be known about Wallace has already been uncovered. Mr Ross has proved that Wallace studies are in fact in their infancy.' ELSPETH KING, Director the the Stirling Smith Art Museum & Gallery, who annotated and introduced the recent Luath edition of *Blind Harry's Wallace*.

'Better the pen than the sword!'

RANDALL WALLACE, author of *Braveheart*, when asked by David Ross how it felt to be partly responsible for the freedom of a nation following the Devolution Referendum.

On the Trail of Robert the Bruce

David R. Ross

ISBN 0 946487 52 9 PBK £7.99

On the Trail of Robert the Bruce charts the story of Scotland's hero-king from his boyhood, through his days of indecision as Scotland suffered under the English yoke, to his assumption of the crown exactly six months after the death of William Wallace. Here is the astonishing blow by blow account of how,

against fearful odds, Bruce led the Scots to win their greatest ever victory. Bannockburn was not the end of the story. The war against English oppression lasted another fourteen years. Bruce lived just long enough to see his dreams of an independent Scotland come to fruition in 1328 with the signing of the Treaty of Edinburgh. The trail takes us to Bruce sites in Scotland, many of the little known and forgotten battle sites in northern England, and as far afield as the Bruce monuments in Andalusia and Jerusalem.

67 places to visit in Scotland and elsewhere.

One general map, 3 location maps and a map of Bruce-connected sites in Ireland.

Bannockburn battle plan.

Drawings and reproductions of rarely seen illustrations.

On the Trail of Robert the Bruce is not all blood and gore. It brings out the love and laughter, pain and passion of one of the great eras of Scottish history. Read it and you will understand why David Ross has never knowingly killed a spider in his life. Once again, he proves himself a master of the popular brand of hands-on history that made *On the Trail of William Wallace* so popular.

'David R. Ross is a proud patriot and unashamed romantic.'

SCOTLAND ON SUNDAY

'Robert the Bruce knew Scotland, knew every class of her people, as no man who ruled her before or since has done. It was he who asked of her a miracle - and she accomplished it.'

AGNES MUIR MACKENZIE

THE QUEST FOR

The Quest for the Celtic Key
Karen Ralls-MacLeod and Ian Robertson
ISBN 1 84282 084 2 PB £7.99

The Quest for the Nine Maidens
Stuart McHardy
ISBN 0 946487 66 9 HB £16.99

The Quest for Charles Rennie Mackintosh
John Cairney
ISBN 1 84282 058 3 HB £16.99

The Quest for Robert Louis Stevenson
John Cairney
ISBN 0 946487 87 1 HB £16.99

ON THE TRAIL OF

On the Trail of the Pilgrim Fathers
J. Keith Cheetham
ISBN 0 946487 83 9 PB £7.99

On the Trail of Mary Queen of Scots
J. Keith Cheetham
ISBN 0 946487 50 2 PB £7.99

On the Trail of John Wesley
J. Keith Cheetham
ISBN 1 84282 023 0 PB £7.99

On the Trail of Robert Burns
John Cairney
ISBN 0 946487 51 0 PB £7.99

On the Trail of Bonnie Prince Charlie
David R Ross
ISBN 0 946487 68 5 PB £7.99

On the Trail of Queen Victoria in the Highlands
Ian R Mitchell
ISBN 0 946487 79 0 PB £7.99

ISLANDS

The Islands that Roofed the World: Easdale, Belnahua, Luing & Seil:
Mary Withall
ISBN 0 946487 76 6 PB £4.99

Rum: Nature's Island
Magnus Magnusson
ISBN 0 946487 32 4 PB £7.95

LUATH GUIDES TO SCOTLAND

The North West Highlands: Roads to the Isles
Tom Atkinson
ISBN 1 84282 086 9 PB £5.99

Mull and Iona: Highways and Byways
Peter Macnab
ISBN 1 84282 089 3 PB £5.99

The Northern Highlands: The Empty Lands
Tom Atkinson
ISBN 1 84282 087 7 PB £5.99

The West Highlands: The Lonely Lands
Tom Atkinson
ISBN 1 84282 088 5 PB £5.99

TRAVEL & LEISURE

Die Kleine Schottlandfibel [Scotland Guide in German]
Hans-Walter Arends
ISBN 0 946487 89 8 PB £8.99

Let's Explore Berwick-upon-Tweed
Anne Bruce English
ISBN 1 84282 029 X PB £4.99

Let's Explore Edinburgh Old Town
Anne Bruce English
ISBN 0 946487 98 7 PB £4.99

Edinburgh's Historic Mile
Duncan Priddle
ISBN 0 946487 97 9 PB £2.99

Pilgrims in the Rough: St Andrews beyond the 19th hole
Michael Tobert
ISBN 0 946487 74 X PB £7.99

NATURAL WORLD

The Hydro Boys: pioneers of renewable energy
Emma Wood
ISBN 1 84282 047 8 PB £8.99

Wild Scotland
James McCarthy
photographs by Laurie Campbell
ISBN 0 946487 37 5 PB £8.99

Wild Lives: Otters – On the Swirl of the Tide
Bridget MacCaskill
ISBN 0 946487 67 7 PB £9.99

Wild Lives: Foxes – The Blood is Wild
Bridget MacCaskill
ISBN 0 946487 71 5 PB £9.99

Scotland – Land & People: An Inhabited Solitude
James McCarthy
ISBN 0 946487 57 X PB £7.99

The Highland Geology Trail
John L Roberts
ISBN 0 946487 36 7 PB £5.99

Red Sky at Night
John Barrington
ISBN 0 946487 60 X PB £8.99

Listen to the Trees
Don MacCaskill
ISBN 0 946487 65 0 PB £9.99

THE QUEST FOR

The Quest for the Celtic Key
Karen Ralls-MacLeod and
Ian Robertson
ISBN 1 84282 084 2 PB £7.99

The Quest for Robert Louis Stevenson
John Cairney
ISBN 1 84282 085 0 PB £8.99

The Quest for Arthur
Stuart McHardy
ISBN 1 84282 012 5 HB £16.99

Tall Tales from an Island
Peter Macnab
ISBN 0 946487 07 3 PB £8.99

The Supernatural Highlands
Francis Thompson
ISBN 0 946487 31 6 PB £8.99

GENEALOGY

Scottish Roots: step-by-step guide for ancestor hunters
Alwyn James
ISBN 1 84282 007 9 PB £9.99

SPORT

Over the Top with the Tartan Army
Andy McArthur
ISBN 0 946487 45 6 PB £7.99

Ski & Snowboard Scotland
Hilary Parke
ISBN 0 946487 35 9 PB £6.99

FICTION

Torch
Lin Anderson
ISBN 1 84282 042 7 PB £9.99

Heartland
John MacKay
ISBN 1 84282 059 1 PB £9.99

The Blue Moon Book
Anne MacLeod
ISBN 1 84282 061 3 PB £9.99

The Glasgow Dragon
Des Dillon
ISBN 1 84282 056 7 PB £9.99

The Fundamentals of New Caledonia
David Nicol
ISBN 1 84282 93 6 HB £16.99

The Road Dance
John MacKay
ISBN 1 84282 024 9 PB £6.99

The Strange Case of RL Stevenson
Richard Woodhead
ISBN 0 946487 86 3 HB £16.99

But n Ben A-Go-Go
Matthew Fitt
ISBN 0 946487 82 0 HB £10.99
ISBN 1 84282 014 1 PB £6.99

The Bannockburn Years
William Scott
ISBN 0 946487 34 0 PB £7.95

Outlandish Affairs: An Anthology of Amorous Encounters
Edited and introduced by Evan Rosenthal and Amanda Robinson
ISBN 1 84282 055 9 PB £9.99

Six Black Candles
Des Dillon
ISBN 1 84282 053 2 PB £6.99

Me and Ma Gal
Des Dillon
ISBN 1 84282 054 0 PB £5.99

POETRY

Burning Whins
Liz Niven
ISBN 1 84282 074 5 PB £8.99

Drink the Green Fairy
Brian Whittingham
ISBN 1 84282 020 6 PB £8.99

Tartan & Turban
Bashabi Fraser
ISBN 1 84282 044 3 PB £8.99

The Ruba'iyat of Omar Khayyam, in Scots
Rab Wilson
ISBN 1 84282 046 X PB £8.99

Talking with Tongues
Brian D. Finch
ISBN 1 84282 006 0 PB £8.99

Kate o Shanter's Tale and other poems [book]
Matthew Fitt
ISBN 1 84282 028 1 PB £6.99

Kate o Shanter's Tale and other poems [audio CD]
Matthew Fitt
ISBN 1 84282 043 5 PB £9.99

Bad Ass Raindrop
Kokumo Rocks
ISBN 1 84282 018 4 PB £6.99

Madame Fifi's Farewell and other poems
Gerry Cambridge
ISBN 1 84282 005 2 PB £8.99

Poems to be Read Aloud
introduced by Tom Atkinson
ISBN 0 946487 00 6 PB £5.00

Scots Poems to be Read Aloud
introduced by Stuart McHardy
ISBN 0 946487 81 2 PB £5.00

Picking Brambles
Des Dillon
ISBN 1 84282 021 4 PB £6.99

Sex, Death & Football
Alistair Findlay
ISBN 1 84282 022 2 PB £6.99

The Luath Burns Companion
John Cairney
ISBN 1 84282 000 1 PB £10.00

Immortal Memories: A Compilation of Toasts to the Memory of Burns as delivered at Burns Suppers, 1801-2001
John Cairney
ISBN 1 84282 009 5 HB £20.00

The Whisky Muse: Scotch whisky in poem & song
Robin Laing
ISBN 1 84282 041 9 PB £7.99

A Long Stride Shortens the Road
Donald Smith
ISBN 1 84282 073 7 PB £8.99

Into the Blue Wavelengths
Roderick Watson
ISBN 1 84282 075 3 PB £8.99

The Souls of the Dead are Taking the Best Seats: 50 World Poets on War
Compiled by Angus Calder and Beth Junor
ISBN 1 84282 032 X PB £7.99

Sun Behind the Castle
Angus Calder
ISBN 1 84282 078 8 PB £8.99

FOOD & DRINK

The Whisky Muse: Scotch whisky in poem & song
various, compiled and edited by Robin Laing
ISBN 1 84282 041 9 PB £7.99

First Foods Fast: how to prepare good simple meals for your baby
Lara Boyd
ISBN 1 84282 002 8 PB £4.99

Edinburgh and Leith Pub Guide
Stuart McHardy
ISBN 0 946487 80 4 PB £4.95

WALK WITH LUATH

Skye 360: walking the coastline of Skye
Andrew Dempster
ISBN 0 946487 85 5 PB £8.99

Walks in the Cairngorms
Ernest Cross
ISBN 0 946487 09 X PB £4.95

Short Walks in the Cairngorms
Ernest Cross
ISBN 0 946487 23 5 PB £4.95

The Joy of Hillwalking
Ralph Storer
ISBN 1 84282 069 9 PB £7.50

Scotland's Mountains before the Mountaineers
Ian R Mitchell
ISBN 0 946487 39 1 PB £9.99

Mountain Days & Bothy Nights
Dave Brown & Ian R Mitchell
ISBN 0 946487 15 4 PB £7.50

Of Big Hills and Wee Men
Peter Kemp
ISBN 1 84282 052 4 PB £7.99

BIOGRAPHY

The Last Lighthouse
Sharma Krauskopf
ISBN 0 946487 96 0 PB £7.99

Tobermory Teuchter
Peter Macnab
ISBN 0 946487 41 3 PB £7.99

Bare Feet & Tackety Boots
Archie Cameron
ISBN 0 946487 17 0 PB £7.95

Come Dungeons Dark
John Taylor Caldwell
ISBN 0 946487 19 7 PB £6.95

SOCIAL HISTORY

Pumpherston: the story of a shale oil village
Sybil Cavanagh
ISBN 1 84282 011 7 HB £17.99
ISBN 1 84282 015 X PB £10.99

Shale Voices
Alistair Findlay
ISBN 0 946487 78 2 HB £17.99
ISBN 0 946487 63 4 PB £10.99

A Word for Scotland
Jack Campbell
ISBN 0 946487 48 0 PB £12.99

Crofting Years
Francis Thompson
ISBN 0 946487 06 5 PB £6.95

Hail Philpstoun's Queen
Barbara and Marie Pattullo
ISBN 1 84282 095 8 PB £6.99

HISTORY

Desire Lines: A Scottish Odyssey
David R Ross
ISBN 1 84282 033 8 PB £9.99

Civil Warrior: extraordinary life & poems of Montrose
Robin Bell
ISBN 1 84282 013 3 HB £10.99

FOLKLORE

Scotland: Myth, Legend & Folklore
Stuart McHardy
ISBN 0 946487 69 3 PB £7.99

Luath Storyteller: Highland Myths & Legends
George W Macpherson
ISBN 1 84282 003 6 PB £5.00

Tales of the North Coast
Alan Temperley
ISBN 0 946487 18 9 PB £8.99

LANGUAGE

Luath Scots Language Learner [Book]
L Colin Wilson
ISBN 0 946487 91 X PB £9.99

Luath Scots Language Learner [Double Audio CD Set]
L Colin Wilson
ISBN 1 84282 026 5 CD £16.99

Luath Press Limited
committed to publishing well written books worth reading

LUATH PRESS takes its name from Robert Burns, whose little collie Luath (Gael.,
swift or nimble) tripped up Jean Armour at a wedding and gave him the chance to
speak to the woman who was to be his wife and the abiding love of his
life. Burns called one of *The Twa Dogs* Luath after
Cuchullin's hunting dog in Ossian's *Fingal*. Luath Press
was established in 1981 in the heart of Burns country,
and is now based a few steps up the road from Burns'
first lodgings on Edinburgh's Royal Mile.
Luath offers you distinctive writing with a hint of
unexpected pleasures.

Most bookshops in the UK, the US, Canada, Australia,
New Zealand and parts of Europe either carry our
books in stock or can order them for you. To order direct
from us, please send a £sterling cheque, postal order, interna-
tional money order or your credit card details (number, address
of cardholder and expiry date) to us at the address below. Please
add post and packing as follows: UK – £1.00 per delivery address;
overseas surface mail – £2.50 per delivery address; overseas air-
mail – £3.50 for the first book to each delivery address, plus £1.00 for each additional
book by airmail to the same address. If your order is a gift, we will happily enclose
your card or message at no extra charge.

Luath Press Limited
543/2 Castlehill
The Royal Mile
Edinburgh EH1 2ND
Scotland
Telephone: 0131 225 4326 (24 hours)
Fax: 0131 225 4324
email: gavin.macdougall@luath.co.uk
Website: www.luath.co.uk